THE STORY BOOK OF EASTBOURNE

WRITTEN BY
ANNALIE SEAMAN

ILLUSTRATED BY
ELLIE FRYER

Foreword

In 2019 I helped to develop an exhibition in which we took iconic objects from Eastbourne's past and attempted to interpret 250 000 years of history in roughly 22 meters of wall space. The approach we took was to weave semi-fictitious accounts of the Town's story around the individual objects – just snippets of a lost time, a glimpse at a possible past, designed to inform, captivate and intrigue. Though successful, I soon saw that we were only scratching the surface, visitors wanted to know more and delve deeper – we had provided an engaging bit of rockpooling but what we needed was a spelunking expedition!

With this, *the Story Book of Eastbourne* was born.

To create such a journey into that unexplored realm of entangled fact and fiction would need an author capable of understanding complex historic and archaeological detail, but who could bring heart, beauty and most importantly, life to cold data - Annalie was the perfect fit.

The best storybooks benefit from pictures and Ellie's illustrative style, combining her love of folklore and nature perfectly reflected the stories' exploration of people and landscape, while not losing the dreamlike feel of an imagined past.

Both Annalie and Ellie were born and grew up in Eastbourne, these are their stories, but they are also yours and mine. Wherever you are from and whoever you are - this is our past, let us explore it together and share in the tears, laughter, drama, intrigue and perhaps, just a touch of magic.

Jonathan Seaman

Contents

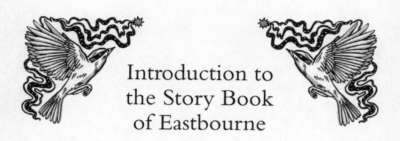

Introduction to the Story Book of Eastbourne

What do a tooth bigger than a human hand, a collection of sharp flints, a morass of Bronze Age timbers, a non-existent Roman villa, two hilltop cemeteries, a tale of two brothers, an Elizabethan manor house and a wheatear pie, a seventeenth century kidnapping, a Georgian court trial, a steam trainline and a flotilla of small boats have in common? They all have something to tell us about the history of Eastbourne.

With this collection of stories, we enter a pre-human world of Pleistocene extinctions and climate change, we consider the first downland farmers, we contemplate Bronze Age sea trade and sea level rise, we explore the edges of the Roman Empire, and look at the landscape evidence for conquest, changing cultures and religions, we discover medieval crime and punishment, and uncover civil rebellion, the woes of empire and piracy, the challenges of post-Napoleonic smuggling and the law, the rapid expansionism of the industrial revolution and the effects of WWII on the inhabitants of the town.

Combined, these stories do more to breathe life into Eastbourne's past than the artefacts, archaeological features and historical documents can do alone. This is a journey of imagination, conjured from the vibrancy and idiosyncrasies of a unique Sussex seaside town. A walk through the modern streets and open landscapes of Eastbourne may help you build up a picture of the history that occurred here, but this group of stories will awaken something else, a curiosity and a wonderment that may just help you imagine the inhabitants of the past as they created history.

"The past, like the future, is indefinite and exists only as a spectrum of possibilities."

Stephen Hawking

The Last Elephant
120,000BCE

During routine excavations in Eastbourne Town Centre, somewhere between South Street and Terminus Road, sometime in the early twentieth century, workmen came across a large, ridged tooth, the size of a man's hand. The odd-looking tooth was sent to experts at the British Museum for further examination. The tooth was categorised as a lower rear molar from a straight-tusked elephant, once extant in this region during the warmer phases of the mid-late Pleistocene epoch. The straight-tusked elephant is now extinct, and this sad, solitary tooth is all we have to remind us of their existence, in the prehistoric wilderness that preceded the birth of Eastbourne town by hundreds of thousands of years.

This story follows the final days of Eastbourne's last elephant, Tusk, as she faces her longest journey, in the memory of her family and the footsteps of her mother.

usk lumbered up the hill one last time and stood facing the sea and the distant lands. The wind brought with it the scents of salt and fish and she breathed in deeply. It could have been the cold wind that made her eyes brim with water, or the touch of ice that blew down from the north.

She remembered running up this hill when she was a calf, her legs spindly and awkward, making her feet choose the wrong directions, so she'd stumble and tumble back down. A strong, grey trunk, thick as an old tree, would reach out for her, rescue her from the fall and tenderly help her right herself. Mama.

There was the wind again, filling her eyes up so that the land around her blurred. For a moment she saw her mama and uncle, her papa and aunties, grandmama and grandpapa, walking proudly in procession ahead of her as she tried to catch up, her legs tangling up beneath her, slowing her down.

Wait, she thought, I'm coming.

But when her eyes cleared, there was no one to be seen.

Tusk had grown strong as her herd dwindled. One by one her family had taken themselves off to the bone field to lie down and sleep. Mama was the last to leave - Tusk had waited a sun's arc before following her there. She found her mama's great grey body lying heavily amongst the bleached bones of their ancestors. Tusk had lain by her side until hunger made her move again.

Fifteen years she'd wandered lonely through the hills and valleys by the shore, meeting rhino-clan and hippo-clan by the water's edge, mooing and honking greetings as she passed. She left the water hole to sleep alone in the valley bottom by the great oak and she woke each sun-up to graze and browse on the foliage that grew a little shorter each year. She wrapped her own trunk, now as broad as her mama's had once been, around her body as she slept and dreamed of her calfhood and the great elephant trail in the sky, where her mama and her family surely roamed each day, following the sun.

Each year came a little darker and a little colder, until Tusk couldn't remember the long hot days of summer she had once known. The hazel and elm trees pined for the sun as she did – this milder sun's warmth never quite made it through her hide. There were fewer maple and oak now than there had been and more grass which was harder to eat and left her hungry. Pine trees were growing up around the edges of the forest, and birches with self-peeling skin, but the needles of the pine scratched her throat, and the birch bark was bitter on her tongue.

Today, the walk up the hill had tired her, and the wind buffeted her body. She yawned. She must walk, she thought, walk on. There was somewhere she needed to be. Her legs guided her back down the hill, through the dwindling forest and across the valley floor, her feet dragging through sticky

ERRATUM

The final paragraph on page 11 should read as follows:

A woman followed, hand in a hand with a child, their bare feet pattered lightly on the ground. They brought with them the scent of far-off lands, echoes of long ago. The child drummed her tiny fists against the trees, hummed a song of dreams and skipped around her mother, searching for mushrooms and herbs, berries, and nuts. The song and the rhythm vibrated downwards, echoing through the earth, whispering into Tusk's ear and Tusk shifted in her sleep.

clay as she followed them through the wetlands and away from the sea.

Oh.

You've brought me here, she thought, as her legs came to stand in the bone field.

She could make out the great white bones laid bare where her mama's great grey body had once lain. Tusk stumbled to her knees, so tired. White bone ribs arched above and around her. I am not old, am I? She thought as she reached her trunk out to rest on her mama's bleached white skull and long, straight tusks.

Wait, Mama, I'm coming.

She closed her eyes and a single tear slid down her cheek and quivered on the tip of her tusk. She wrapped her trunk around her shoulder, like the caress of her mama, and felt the sun shine wanly on her tired body. As she closed her eyes, she saw her uncles and her papa, her aunties and grandpapa, and her mama and grandmama walk towards her and beckon her to join them on the endless trail.

Tusk slept and as she slept, the land grew colder, dusting her slumbering body with drifts of snow. Rhino and hippo and deer came to sleep with her, and the sun arced, leading the moon and the stars and the spirits of the animals through the eternal skies.

Many thousands of years passed in this way as night followed day and vast forests of pine and birch surrounded Tusk and her ancestors. Rain and wind bleached her bones and leaves fell and covered her. Plants and flowers curled to dust and their soils buried her. Cocooned by the earth, Tusk slept on, and the earth rose above her, high and higher still.

The sun grew warmer and hotter, and the rains fell. Roots of birch and pine crumbled, and other seeds filtered down through the earth, seeds of oak and elm, of hazel and maple and they burst wide open, and their roots snaked low and tickled Tusk's cheek and their stalks grew tall and the land above her changed again.

Who can say how many thousands of years she lay there, below the pine forests and oak forests? The stars did not keep count, nor did the sea nor the sun or moon. But many, many years did pass. Many, many thousands.

One day, a man came, tall on two legs, flint spear in hand. He stalked the woods above Tusk, searching for deer and boar. His bare feet tapped on the forest floor, vibrations rippling through tree roots deep down into the earth where she lay sleeping, gently rocking.

A woman followed, hand in a hand with a child, their bare feet pattered

The Shepherd's Gaze
1895CE

Shepherd Blackmore spent countless hours guiding flocks of sheep across the Downs of Eastbourne and East Dean. Along the way, he collected hundreds of Neolithic flint tools, a collection he built-on, cherished and later donated to the Sussex Archaeological Society. He kept behind a small chest of his favourite pieces, which he sometimes showed to visitors of great and small renown. The Downland pastures, that the shepherd roamed, retained Neolithic earthworks and the hidden archaeology of the late Stone Age. We discover in his flint collection, and the biographical accounts of the people he met, an evocative discourse on the past landscape of Beachy Head, and the Downland inhabitants of the past.

The following story gives us a glimpse into the life of the Shepherd of Beachy Head, and for a while, we can join him in his gaze across the years, back in time to the Neolithic period and Eastbourne's first farmers.

ime-crows had been pecking at the corners of Stephen's eyes ever since he took to working the hills and dales of Beachy Head. Relentless sun, sea-blasted winds and driving rains had furrowed his features until he was as carved and weathered as the rocks beneath his feet. His cheeks were raised and contoured like the ancient mounds he climbed, his eyes held a shade of blue that mirrored the sea and sky he gazed upon, ripples ringed his mouth and brow like hollows encircling time-worn embankments.

His craggy, weathered face was framed by a short grey beard and a tall felt hat. Solid, he seemed, strong and constant, slightly buckled by his years, yet there was a kindness about him. His black jacket hung buttoned about his neck like a cape, and under this he wore a simple smock, and trousers. In his hand he held a long crook, iron-topped and hazel-hafted.

If the landscape of this blustery clifftop had etched its mark on Stephen Blackmore's person, so too had he and his sheep carved their marks upon the Downs of Eastbourne and East Dean. Paths worn through to chalk marked sinuous lines from cottage to cliff, through hill and vale, past grass shorn short year-round. A visitor could tell where Shepherd Blackmore and his flock had been.

He had not known a day's leave since he moved to the flint cottage on the Downs. For Stephen, life was an eternal round of walking and gazing, up and down with the sun, led here and there by hundreds of bleating sheep. Alongside him, ran his aged old collie, raised, and trained by Stephen from a pup. Now Shep was blind with the years and workworn enough to have earned his place in rest by the fire, but the urge to roam lingered in the dog as in the man and they rambled together, carving subtle tracks into the slopes. Though age had carved its solemn mark upon the pair, their spirits had grown stronger with the years.

Daily solitude and constant motion had engendered in Stephen a gentle reverie of spirit. His mind easily roamed from the views around him to the time before him when men had carved their tools from the stones of the cliffs. Stephen knew that the mounds he climbed had once held the bones of those who dwelled upon the hills in times long past, in antiquity, those in the know told him. And he knew plenty of men who knew plenty of interesting things. But then, Shepherd Blackmore knew plenty of interesting things too, like where to find the best Neolithic arrowheads and axes on the Downs.

He whistled his dog a well-used tune and set off down the slope. The soil was dry and dusty. They were in need of a good spell of rain. The wind, tempered for once, lifted little whirls of dust and spun them around on the path in front of him.

"A pleasant breeze, is it not?" The man approaching Stephen was well-dressed and -heeled and had the air of one at ease with himself. He strode up the slope towards him, joining him at his vantage overlooking the channel.

"Aye." Stephen replied, "but you would not call it pleasant sir, if you was up here sometimes in the winter." He remembered the snows that'd come late this year, burying the early spring flowers under drifts of whiteness. The sheep had tramped little hoofed prints through the snow as they pushed it aside in search of grass. Snowdrops, preserved for a time in the shock of the freeze, soon withered as the snows melted. Stephen's toes had remained frost-nipped for most of March. He winced slightly at the memory.

Arthur was his name, the man told the shepherd, of the Beckett family of newspaper men, who ran the local *Herald*. He was taken, he said, with the idea of writing a book about the 'Spirit of the Downs' - as if there was something about the landscape that could be caught in print. He asked Stephen about his years as a shepherd. Stephen, happy for the company, remarked that he'd never had a day off sick in his life, except for the time he lost his hand. That took Arthur aback - he gazed uncertainly at the empty smock-sleeve swinging by Shepherd Blackmore's side. Got most people, that did. Stephen allowed himself a chuckle. He no longer cared about the day the chaff-cutter had taken his arm clean-off, but he did enjoy other people's reactions.

They strolled along amiably enough, Arthur asking his questions about the shepherd's life as if he'd never encountered a shepherd before. Stephen listened and responded to questions about his wages – not much changed since the time of Waterloo – and his family. It was hard to bring up memories of his lost daughters and son, gone before they'd made it out of childhood. Two surviving lads had grown strong though, and now mithered at him to slow down, to hang up his crook and smock and respect his age.

Stephen stopped to pick up a stone, flat and smooth, glinting in the sun. He ran his finger over the cool, patterned surface, checking its edges for serrations and sharpness, casting his eye over ripples and grooves, and rubbing his thumb across the contours. It felt wrong, ridged where the ridge held no use, cracked where the stone had been exposed to frost and ice. It didn't have the shape of something useful - nor the feel of something that fitted to his grip. He tossed it back to the grass and carried on his way, his eyes scanning the ground, the landscape, counting-up his herd.

"What's that you found there?" Arthur asked.

"I thought it were an old arrowhead," Stephen replied. "There are hundreds on these Downs if you know how to find them. I've got a tidy few at home."

Arthur expressed a desire to see them, and Stephen invited him to the cottage to take a look. They followed the sheep to their fold and Arthur watched on as the Shepherd and his dog guided the sheep through the gate. They climbed Frost Hill, their backs to the sea, and approached the Shepherd's cottage, a well-worn house of flint and brick, its little garden blooming with cabbages and potato plants. They stepped inside and Stephen called out to his wife that they had a guest come to see his stones. Maria appeared at the kitchen door, wisps of white hair escaping from under a frilled bonnet, her hands wet from some chore. She nodded and watched the men climb the stairs.

Stephen took Arthur to a room piled high with drawers and chests. He took some boxes carefully down and showed the contents to Arthur. Axe-heads, arrowheads, points, scrapers and picks, and shapes carved from flint, sat beautifully in their trays. Arthur admired the relics, as he called them, of the long past, though Stephen could tell that the newspaperman was struggling to imagine the time that had passed between then and now. Perhaps he just didn't know how to gaze backwards.

"They were drawn these ones, by a man from the *Society*," Stephen said, indicating a selection of tools. "Published them he did. Though I think he did that for his own ends rather than mine. Mr. Charles Dawson, he were, funny fellow."

Arthur remarked that he knew of him and said no more than that. He wanted to know who else had been interested in Stephen's stones. "Oh, that Thomas Huxley had an interest." Stephen replied. "He were a great man Sir, though I never heard tell of what he did." He gazed off out the window, as if searching for a memory. "He did have a fondness for talking of dinosaurs and birds. Been to Australia, he had… all the way round the world… and he spoke well of his good friend Mr. Darwin, he was a Charles too." Stephen shook his head sadly. "Gone too soon, Mr. Huxley was, hadn't lived in these parts more than five years before the Lord took him off."

Arthur marvelled at Stephen's varied stories of learned men who roamed these hills, learning how to gaze. He praised the Shepherd's collection, wondering what would become of them in the end. "Oh, they'll be going to the Society in Lewes." Stephen told him. "Got a fine collection of artefacts, they have, and these'll be taken good care of there. Well, most of them." His eyes flicked to a wooden chest that held pride of place on a cabinet. "Some I won't be giving away."

Stephen had a lot to think about over the next few days; his memories had been all stirred up, especially images of his lost daughters. He couldn't walk far or fast enough away from his churning thoughts. As he part-led, part-followed his flock over hills and hollows, pausing every now and then to scan the horizon, the wide blue sea, and folded green hills, he found himself returning to a gentle reverie that suited him better.

It so happened that at the precise moment when a quietness of spirit settled around him again, he noticed a shaped flint on the ground ahead. He stooped to pick it up and connected, with a start, to something much older than him. The flint was carved, intricately so, pale and patterned by the years, its edges dulled by soil and chalk. It sat on his palm, a triangular tribute to its maker, an old hunter long gone. Ripples and waves marked its surface, struck upon the stone, blow by blow until its shape had emerged, slender as a pine, sharp as a thorn. A weapon to fell a beast.

It would have been easy for him to imagine that little had changed on Beachy Head in all these years, but he knew different. He had a fine set of books - weighty things that spoke of long ago, of the early days of the world - and this, combined with a deep sense of knowing, led Shepherd Blackmore to well imagine the lives of the first shepherds of Beachy Head.

His stones, most of them, had come from Neolithic people, those who had come after the first men – those Palaeolithic ones - with their rude stone tools. Stephen wasn't nearly as interested in them, though he'd collected a few anyhow. With his books, his discussions and his keen eye for discovery and collection, he had learned the tale of Beachy Head's prehistoric peoples. He saw their traces in the turf-covered chalk mounds and earthworks, found their cunning in the tools and weapons they had left behind. He knew of the days before the Neolithic peoples, of the days when men knew nothing of agriculture, when old, wild forest filled the land, and the seas lapped a further shore, when men hunted for their meat and foraged for their fruits.

It was more than time that had changed that. The oceans had swelled up, turning Britain into an island, the summers had gotten warmer, and the Neolithic peoples had learned to farm animals and grow crops. They'd changed the land around them, cleared its trees, planted their wheat and peas, and fenced their livestock in. They'd built their long homes of wood and clay under a treeless sky and moulded the land to suit them.

The forests had been steadily cleared over time and they raised their earthworks up on the highest hills, with ramparts and ditches like ancient castles. Stephen reasoned that those first farmers - men, women, and children - had moved around the landscape, taking advantage of the bounties of sea, river, and forest, retreating to their hilltop palisades only when danger or occasion demanded.

He knew where they'd roamed, knew the views they'd encountered, knew what their gazes had been drawn to: the wide blue sea and folded green hills. Though his meat came packaged from the butcher's and his milk from the dairy, his vegetables and fruit from Eastbourne market and his beer from the local brewery, that didn't mean that Shepherd Blackmore hadn't worked out a thing or two about how a Neolithic-type might have produced their food. There would have been unfarmed food too, he reasoned. Even he knew of the migrations of the fish and shelled creatures of the shore; he knew where the birds of land and coast nested; he knew when and where the berries and nuts erupted from the plants; and he knew about the deer and boar that used to roam these parts, when the forest still stood. If he knew this, he could be sure that those who'd lived here before him would have known this and so much more.

Stephen knew where flint stones could be collected from the cliffs and beach - from the clay-with-flints buried below the turf - where the best nodules could be extracted from. He'd had a go himself, at knocking shapes into flint. He wasn't skilled at it, hadn't put the time in, but he knew at least he was capable of it. It gave a man a great deal of respect for an ancestor who could achieve such feats of creation with flint and tine as those he'd collected on his way. He was under no illusion that Neolithic meant primitive. There was a strength and skill in living from the land, skill that Shepherd Blackmore didn't have.

Of course, he knew more than most, of the seasons on the hills, of the winds and storms that drive the flints from the cliffs, of mists that cling to the slopes like clouds. He knew more than most, of the seasons of a shepherd, one who keeps his flock close at heel, of the rhythm of the growing year and the harvest. Shepherd Blackmore knew when things had changed for the first farmers, he knew that once they'd succeeded in taming their sheep and goats, their giant cows, their plants, he knew that was the moment they stopped roaming free and started changing the world.

Everything around him showed how far people had come since those early days of innovation: the great towns and railways, planes and guns, electricity, and coal. They had all developed, he knew, from the pioneering imaginations of those first farmers, like the ones who tended the first sheep on Beachy Head.

What would people know of the past in a hundred years? He wondered. Was there more to learn or was it all known already? Was it, as he suspected, so obvious in its simplicity as to merit no further ponderance?

Stephen Blackmore didn't know. He pocketed his new flint and guided the sheep back home, whistling the usual trills and tweeps to the old boy, and the blue sky, as they climbed and descended the undulating sward.

River's Reflection
810BCE

I n the September of 1995, in a soggy trench in the Shinewater marsh at Langney, several ancient timbers were discovered, alongside well-preserved artefacts of exquisite rarity. Bronze axes from Holland, amber beads from the Baltic region, and shale bracelets from Dorset, lay preserved in the oxygen-free environment, along with a hafted bronze sickle, complete with its wooden handle, and other fine examples of bronze tools, lead jewellery and carved bridle-pieces. The archaeologists had uncovered the remains of a Late Bronze Age settlement with wooden trackways extending across the marsh. Subsequent environmental investigations in the area, revealed a changing Bronze Age and Iron Age landscape of wetland, estuary, salt flats, rivers, streams, and marine inundations. Amongst the water-logged finds, a human burial and several other disarticulated human bones were found, in the vicinity of the main platform. The people of the Bronze Age Shinewater settlement appear to have practised a particular type of watery burial rite, in the liminal space between wet and dry land.

This story follows the trials of a young Bronze Age girl and her family living in the flooded wetlands as the climate deteriorates and the marsh begins to disappear beneath the sea.

ain fell sideways, driven by a coastal wind that whipped the marsh reeds and sedges into an agitated frenzy. River clutched her brother's hand tighter and hurried them along the trackway, their feet slapping in salty water as they crossed the estuary, toes slipping on sunken hazel rods, the oak posts lost somewhere beneath the lapping tide. Their dog, Hunter, splashed across the track ahead of them, his gaze returning to them beseechingly as the wind stirred wildly and they stumbled onwards.

"Come on now, Beck, let's hurry. Mama's waiting for us."

"But River, I'm so tired."

"I know little one, me too." And she was. In all her twelve years, River had never known such tiredness, it was as relentless as the wintry rains, as the short, grey days and dull grey sky. Even the marsh was grey, reflecting the gloom that fell from above. She carried a pair of collared doves by their necks. Beck had tried shooting again today, but his aim was less than true, his feet heavy on the ground. He'd startled the last deer from River's sight, she'd loosed the arrow anyhow, but it had glanced off a tree instead of the animal's flank and splintered into pieces. These doves would have to do, River thought, not that the meat would fill their bellies for long. The winter stores were low, badly so, stored grains lost to the rising tide, and the blossoming season was slow to appear.

The marsh in high-season was a land of plenty, where their aurochs and sheep grazed, and fish and eels swam between the rushes; where woodcocks *pwee-whipped* and white-tailed eagles soared above the twitter, chirrup, and honk of the birds of marsh and wood, where deer and boar grazed among the border-woods. It was hard to be hungry in high season.

Even the waning days held bounty, when the trees turned bronze and gold, and berries grew, and nuts formed on oak and hazel. The trackways then, rose above the water, well they used to. These last few dark seasons, since grandfather had gone, had grown wetter and wetter, as the sea lapped closer, and the rivers rose higher, and the colours of the seasons had faded to a muted grey. Half the year now, the trackways sunk below the rising tides and the marsh transformed into a wide, clear lake, reflecting endless, shifting rains and bruised clouds heavy with thunder.

The wetlands led out to the wide, salty sea and the promise of lands beyond sight. River often told Beck that they were the betweeners; they weren't people of the land or the river or the sea, they were of all of them and none of them, out here in the place where land and water fought for supremacy.

Their crop fields surrounded the wetlands, rising high up the hill slopes but not so far as the ancestral grounds – they were quiet, past places now. The round barrows of old sat serenely across the upper slopes, alongside the long mounds and enclosures of the ancient ones. The barrow-mounds, glimpsed along the skyline of the long hills, had a melancholy beauty to them, held a remembering of what once was; memories of the people who had walked this land before them, whose blood ran in their veins. They no longer laid their dead to rest in the mounds; they offered them to the spirits of the marsh and the swirling waters instead, offerings to appease the angry skies.

Marsh water lapped against the oak posts and the platform beneath their hut, edging towards the door in sullen, foam-flecked waves.

"Mama, we're home!" River called, pushing the door inwards. The house was cold and dark, water dripped from the reed-thatch and pooled on rush-mats below, droplets splashed on the hearthstone, speckling yesterday's ash, and burnt-out ends of blackened logs. Hunter shook himself out, beads of marsh water spraying the wattled walls. River shivered and sent him to his basket with a strip of dried deer-meat and pulled Beck inside, fastening the door closed and pulling at Beck's clothes. "Come on now, take it off, its dripping." Beck lifted his arms up and let River pull the wet, woollen tunic over his head. His little body, dotted with goosebumps, seemed so small in the half-light of their home. She pulled a blanket from their bed and wrapped him up in it, held him tight, rubbing his back and arms.

"Mama.. are you awake?" a slight groan came from Anahita's bed. "Mother, we've brought doves for you and the baby. Let's light a fire, shall we?" She gathered a small pile of crisp leaves, bark shavings and spindly sticks and sat them on the hearthstone, retrieved the flint and red-stone and struck them together. One strike for the rain, two strikes for her useless mother, three strikes for her shivering brother, four strikes for her missing father, five strikes for her quarrelling uncles, six strikes for her useless aunts, seven strikes… the shavings smouldered under a tiny red spark. River carefully blew on the smoking shavings, added some dry tinder, and coaxed the embers to a flame. Instructing Beck to tend the fire and start plucking the birds. River went to her mother, felt her brow, which had no heat upon it, stroked her pale cheek and pulled her face round until their eyes met, but her mother's held no welcoming glow. She pulled the covers down and felt her mother's domed belly, it rippled faintly, and she felt a tiny kick. Satisfied, she pulled the covers back up and sat by the bed. She'd helped her mother deliver Beck in this very space at the centre of the marsh, nearly six years ago, looked after him ever since, as her mother grew large and small again, over, and over, but never welcoming another child. This one had come further than any of the others, had more life in it, but it was feeble. She'd cupped her aunt's bellies as they grew and swelled and the strength of the kicks inside them had amazed her. Her cousins grew up around her, like slender reeds, while her own siblings shrivelled away to nothing.

It was the curse, they whispered behind her mama's back – sent by River's grandfather because his son had wedded an outsider from another shore with no family of her own, nor wealth or land. That was why her father never stayed home, they said, because grandfather's spirit had banished him from the homelands. River told them that was nonsense, her grandfather had loved her and Beck, and her parents, wouldn't hurt them. But all the same, the rains hadn't stopped since grandfather had passed and the floods rose higher every year, and no siblings had come to help her tend the animals or crops. Beck was useless on the hunt and her papa hadn't returned for nine moons. If this was a curse, then it was a strong one.

"Will you eat mother?" River handed her a bowl of roasted dove, but her mother turned her face away. River sighed and held a cup of water to her mouth, let the clear drops trickle through her cracked lips. Mother licked her lips drily, swallowed a tiny swallow.

River huddled Beck to her and let his warm head rest on her shoulder, his breathing grew rhythmic and slow, and she felt her own eyelids flutter. Is it true, grandfather? She asked silently to the night, as her eyelids grew heavier still, have you cursed us? The wind sighed in answer and River fell to dreaming.

Her feet swiftly stepped barefoot over leaf and grass and hill until she was standing by the ancestor mounds, her hair blowing all about. The wind whipped around her in white fury and through the mist she saw faces, old faces from days long-past of people she'd never known, her father's people, her grandmother, they glared at her, their mouths issuing silent words and they pointed out to sea and up at the clouds and slowly raised their hands, then beckoned for her to look out towards the upper marsh and the sunset hills, and as one, they shoved her towards the setting sun.

Aunt Breda came in the morning, a hard loaf of bread in her hand. River's cousins stood fussing at the door, they'd been told not to ask questions, River could tell, and it irked her that they did as they were told. Who was going to ask her how she was, she wanted to know, as her aunt bent briefly over her mother before placing the bread down and moving to leave? A tender hug would help, a gentle caress, but Breda was too scared of the shadows, thought they'd come for her if she touched the curse-afflicted. Stupid woman. Breda's husband, River's father's brother, was away trading along the coast with his other brother and some men from the hill village. It was tin they were after this time, from the distant sunset lands out to the west, to trade with the copper-merchants from beyond the wide sea. They would come home, her aunt assured her, because they'd married well – no curse on them, see? River didn't see. She'd come back later to check on Anahita, Breda said, which was nothing to River, but drips from a leaky cup.

Come home father. Please. River beseeched the wide grey waters and the wide grey sky.

Grandfather's skull gleamed whitely from the post at the centre of the house platform. Grandfather had helped build the wooden trackways and platform to keep their access to the crop fields clear when the waters rose; to help the trading-boats dock at the river's edge. The very earth and water around the track and platform were bounded with parts of him and his people, with their long bones which had been offered to the waters, with his old bronze knife, and other fine bronze gifts, sent down to the shadow world with them. River's father had placed Grandfather's skull high on the ancestor post, where he could sightlessly watch over them all. It mattered where they'd come from, who their people were, River's father had told her. It mattered that they remembered them. What about mother? River had asked, does it matter who her people were? Of course, her father had replied, but she's one of us now, she's of this land, as are you.

High season had been short the year before, the autumn floods, early and long-lived, had eventually receded until the wetlands held a mingling of salt marsh, mud flats, bogs, river channels and pools of salt-and-fresh water where the stream met the tide. Now the spring tides were upon them and this year they showed no sign of waning. Beyond the house platform, a little dug-out canoe bobbed on the flood and their oxcart had disappeared beneath the waters, though one of its timber handles still speared the surface.

She found Beck outside by the ancestor-post, sitting cross-legged on the oaken planks of the house platform, which today seemed more like a raft, as marsh water slapped soundly against the underside of the planks. He was gazing up at their grandfather's skull and winding some nettle cord around a white eagle feather and a black flint knife. He was chanting softly, his lips forming whispered words. River sat with him. He finished winding the cord and set the bundle down in an earthen pot at the pillar's base. When he was done, he turned to River and smiled a thin smile.

"Grandfather came to me in my dreams, River. I told him I'd sing for him and remember him."

"What does he look like in your dreams?"

"Tall, and streak-haired, like a heron, with dark eyes and eagle feathers braided in his hair."

"That is how he was, Beck! You see him true."

Beck stared up at the skull, his head cocked to one side. "Where's the rest of him?" He asked, his doe-brown eyes wide with wonder.

"He broke apart when his spirit left his body, Beck, we talked about it before, remember?"

"But where did it go?"

"His spirit? Back to the sky. His flesh returned to the earth, his bones to the water, ready to create new life. That's how all life is Beck, it forms and dissolves and forms again."

Beck looked out over the water, watching the sky reflected upside-down on the glossy surface below, so he saw two worlds looking back at him.

"Will I die too?" Beck asked.

River hugged him close. "Yes, little one, but not for many, many years. See here..." River crouched down at the edge of the platform and looked at her own face gazing back at her. Beck's reflection joined hers on the surface of the water. Behind their mirrored faces, grey clouds scudded by. "Look at your image here, it is just your image today. Tomorrow you will not be the same, you'll be older, taller. By the end of your days, you won't remember how this face of yours looks today." River wiggled her fingers in the water and their faces disappeared among rings of ripples. "One day beyond that, the water won't remember your face either and you will be beyond the light."

"Down in the shadows? With Grandfather?"

"Yes!" River laughed, "if you like. But do not ask where you will go when you die, little one." River tousled Beck's hair and stroked his smooth cheek. "Ask instead where you came from before you were born, that is where you will return to, and it is nothing to fear."

The ripples bled outwards, becoming absorbed in the stillness of the waters of the marsh, before heading out to join the turbulent waves of the oceans beyond the wetlands.

"River?"

"Yes?"

"Is that what happened to mama's babies? They didn't want to come here - they wanted to stay where they were?"

River sighed. "You're right Beck, they didn't want to come. Maybe this one..." Her words trailed off across the estuary, convincing neither of them.

Mama was moaning as they entered their home, weary fear brimming at the moist corners of her eyes, her hands clutching her belly.

Last year – River remembered the same scene – her mama moaning on the bed, her papa missing, trading in some far-distant lands. There had been blood, so much blood, and screams and a tiny, lifeless babe clutched in her mama's arms, reddened tears streaking her face. Then silence and rain.

They'd offered the tiny thing to the birds of the marsh and its bones to the marshy silts beneath their house, along with the others who'd never learnt to breathe. Surely, they had paid enough in sacrifice already. This child *could come, could* grow with Beck and River - fill their home with laughter.

"I'm here mama.. how is the baby?" She walked swiftly over to Anahita, cupped her forehead, her belly. Her mother moaned again, "You're alright, mama. I am here."

River sponged cool water on her mama's forehead and sung to her, a stream of melodies from her childhood. The tunes soothed Anahita and she closed her eyes, breathing softly, lulled to sleep.

"Beck, are you there?" Beck came to stand by River. "It's alright, mama's alright." River whispered and held her hand out to him. "You can sit with me or go to the aunts?"

"You, I'll stay with you." He reached out for her hair, twining it round his fingers as he'd done as a toddler. "Tell me a story River?" He pleaded.

"Alright, which one?"

"The wolf-blade of Scheldt-land? Tell me that one!"

"Again?"

"Again."

River pulled Beck onto her lap and cuddled him close, one hand resting on her mother's belly and the hidden babe within. "Far away and many moons ago, there was a mighty smith who forged a magical sword." Beck grinned up at her, nodding. "The Smith of Scheldt-land built up his fire so high, wood upon wood, and he coaxed the flames with the bellows, and he melted the earth-metals so hot that the tin-blood ran free like liquid silver, but still the copper wouldn't soften, and he pumped the fire hotter and hotter through day and dusk, and a full moon rose in the sky and all was calm and still, just the whoosh-and-wheesh of air bellowing the fire."

"Go on."

"And the tin-blood bubbled away but the copper stayed firm, and he was tired from all his work and nearly out of strength and then..."

"Go on... go on!" Beck squirmed on her lap, jiggling with excitement.

"...a wolf appeared in the flames..."

"No!"

"Yes! The fiery face of a glowing wolf. The fire-wolf howled and licked the flames with his red tongue and the fire came hotter and hotter until out of nowhere, the fire-wolf summoned the sky-fires and lightning struck the ground right next to the smith." Beck nearly leapt from her lap, arcing his arm down like the bearer of lightning. ". .and the flames roared, and the copper melted, and its golden-blood blended with the silvery tin-blood, pooling together into bronze, and the smith poured it swiftly into the blade-mould and he knew, as the liquid metal hardened into shape, that it was the finest blade he'd ever made - The Wolf-Blade from the Smith of Scheldt-land."

Beck got up and walked over to the oaken chest. "And this is the very one?" he asked in wonder as he pulled the bronze blade from its scabbard.

"The very one. Papa traded wool and tin for it and brought the blade home over all the lands and streams and oceans between us. He brought it home for our protection."

"It will die with him?"

"No, not this one, Beck. He brought it back for you."

"What if he is dead already?"

"He's not, I know it."

Mama woke quickly, urged from within. River greeted her softly and sent Beck for some water.
"You'll have to boil it Beck, light the fire like I showed you."

Anahita bore the intensity of the pulsing tides that flowed through her, as the light faded from the sky and her groans rent the strained silence of the darkening marsh, River coaxing her, Beck clutching her hand. Night fell a dusky grey, streaked with orange-fire. Through the darkness, they held each other, as the moon ascended, and pale stars winked in their thousands from an eerily clear sky. The baby came at last, fragile, and blue-tinged. *Not again!* River thought, blinking back tears. She took the baby in her arms and rubbed its tiny back, held his tiny body upside-down, cleared his mouth, rubbed, and rubbed, blew her breath into his mouth: the breath of life.

The baby coughed and gargled, an eye flickered, unfocused blue, and then a wail tore from his tiny mouth, setting the marsh birds a-flutter. He suckled at his mama's breast. Mama, smiling wanly, dozed on and off with the baby in her arms.

The next day he was still there. Another night and day passed, and he lived. As he drew life from Anahita, her hunger came, and she began to take the food they offered.

A moon passed and the boy swelled strong.

"It's time to name him." Anahita said, as the buds swelled on the trees and the plants all around them ripened into life.

"What, mama? What's he to be called?" River asked, cradling her brother.

"Okeah for his father, the one who moves with water."

Mama sat weaving by the hearth as the baby slept, singing softly to Beck who sat at her feet. Hunter slept soundly by them as a flat bread baked on the stone and a fresh-caught fish sizzled on a spit above the fire.

Barley and emmer were growing well in their fields, as were the peas and flax. Their cattle, sheep and pigs were back from the pasture and River had a good feeling about this year. Mama smiled and sparkled, joy lifting her from the shadows, and she told them of the time she met their papa on the river by her home village, far off in the sun-lands.

"…Perhaps he is with my people now, remembering us," a shadow flickered across her eyes. "All I have of my people now are memories."

"And stories, Mama," River said. "Tell us of the horses."

"Such beautiful creatures. I had my own horse, Parthia, she was pure black from nose to tail and as tall as I am now."

"And you rode on her back?"

"Of course, that was our way."

"What of the sun horse, Mama?" Beck asked.

"Well now, the Sun Horse is a mighty horse indeed. He pulls the sun from east to west across the sky on a golden chariot and when he reaches the edge of the world, he descends to the shadowy underworld where he runs through darkness until he reaches the other side."

"…and the sun horse taught you to ride?"

"He taught my people. He taught us how to fix ropes around our horses' heads without harming them and how to leap upon their backs and steer their course. He taught us how to make wheels in the shape of the sun for our earth-chariots and how to charm oxen to pull our ploughs and carts."

"Will we ever have a horse Mama?" River asked.

"I hope so. Perhaps that is what is keeping your papa from us now, maybe he is bringing a horse home for us."

The marsh-waters receded, though not as much as they used to. The seas were rising, and change was blowing through. There were whispers of it in the skies. They shouldn't stay there another dark season; River was sure of it. They had to move, before the nights grew too long. Anahita urged the council – still short of men – and begged them all to rethink their futures. They could move upland, Anahita said, she knew a place at the high edge of the marsh where the waters never reached, where they would be safe from the surging tides. And the aunts listened and fretted and were led less by reason than by fear. They would have to learn the slow way.

Beck grew swifter and stealthier-at-hunt day by day, and Okeah was hungry for life. Anahita, River and Beck, and eventually Okeah, would work the fields together, move the livestock to higher ground, where the water wouldn't rot their hooves. They'd build a new house from the shell of the old, convince the others to join them, with or without the men. River would wait for her father to return across the ocean, and when he came, he'd find them in a fine new settlement above the water, but not far from it. They'd take grandfather's skull with them, but leave the other bones and the old ways, leave them for the water. They'd begin anew, on the upper edges of the western marsh; say goodbye to eel and beaver, to otter, stoat, and mallard, and seek their place among the creatures of the land, leaving the turbulent waters to the elements, the spirits, and the ancestors.

Villa: Conversations
2021 CE

I t has long been known that a Roman villa once existed on the seafront in Eastbourne, joining this part of Britain with the Roman Empire. Roman Eastbourne itself is an elusive entity. Only scattered remains of a once vibrant society have been located across the town. A Roman settlement once thrived on the edge of the marsh, where industrial salt making took place. Roman fields were worked on the slopes of the Downs, and a seemingly isolated farmstead existed at Bullock Down. Roman burials have been discovered on the Downland slopes at Meads and Old Town, and on the valley slope above East Dean. They were here, the Romans, but unusually for that period, their trace is slight and ephemeral. A thin archive of documentary evidence exists to show us the dimensions and location of Eastbourne's seafront Roman villa, but the archive is incomplete. Which leaves us to wonder just what can be learned about Eastbourne's Roman past.

The following story is based on conversations between a mother and her children as they work through the evidence and to try and imagine what the Eastbourne Roman villa might have been like.

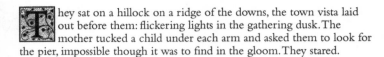

hey sat on a hillock on a ridge of the downs, the town vista laid out before them: flickering lights in the gathering dusk. The mother tucked a child under each arm and asked them to look for the pier, impossible though it was to find in the gloom. They stared.

"Over there, in the hump." Lyra pointed.

"No, over there in the dip!" Rhys pointed.

"In front of me?" The mother asked.

"No, in front of me." The children chorused.

Yet still it could not be agreed upon whether the thing had been found or not. It was a moot point.

"What would it mean to you if I said there was a Roman villa down there?"

"Where?"

"By the pier."

"Can we go and see it?"

"What does it look like?"

"It's not there anymore, it fell into the sea."

"Let's look for it under the sea then." Rhys said, excitedly.

"No, it crumbled into the sea like rubble. There'd be nothing to find by now."

"How does anyone know it was there then?"

"Others found it, they wrote about it, drew it."

"They could have been lying."

"Yeah, they could have just said there was something there to make money." Lyra added.

"They wouldn't have made any money out of it - and these were good people – trusted."

"I don't believe it."

"No?"

"No, me either."

"What if you saw some parts of it? Tiles – a statue."

"What kind of statue?"

"A little bronze god."

"Where is it?

"Can we see it?"

"Well, it's in Canada."

"Canada?"

"Yes, it was donated by a fellow who wrote about the villa."

"Why Canada?"

"Beats me."

"So, we can't see that."

"No, not really, I mean – you could see a photo."

"Photos are alright I suppose. But how could they know they had the statue from Eastbourne?"

"Yeah, they might not even know where Eastbourne is if they're in Canada."

"Perhaps."

"What else did you say?"

"Tiles?"

"Yes, tiles."

"They're not interesting. There's tiles everywhere around town and no one cares about them."

"Tiles on our house."

"Yes. But these tiles are old."

"How old?"

"2,000 years."

"That's old."

"Yeah."

"Where are they?"

"The tiles? In storage."

"Why?"

"Well, they're part of the collection that makes up the physical past of our town."

"Like a museum?"

"Yes, like a museum."

"A museum in boxes?"

"Yes."

"From the villa that fell into the sea?"

"Yes."

"Can we see them?"

"I expect we could try."

"Cool."

"Yeah, that would be cool."

"So how does it feel to have had a Roman villa in our town?"

"But there is no villa."

"No, well – there might be. They found some of it when they were building the roads and the hotels down on the seafront."

"Did they?"

"Yes. And before that, they found some of it crumbling on the cliff edge."

"Who did?"

"People – historians, archaeologists, antiquarians."

"They could have just said they found it."

"Yeah and made it sound like they knew loads of stuff."

"Some people might do that I guess, but not all of them. They had their reputations to consider."

"They did?"

"They did. They wanted people to trust them and think that they were knowledgeable."

"So they wouldn't have wanted to be called liars."

"No."

"That would have been bad for them."

"They wanted to tell the truth."

"The truth as they saw it, yes. Some of them already knew about the Romans and their villas, the building materials, pottery, and coins."

"There were coins?"

"Yes."

"Can we see them?"

"No, they're lost."

"So, someone did make money out of the villa."

"Maybe, or maybe they just got lost."

"I lose things." Rhys said.

"So do I." Lyra added.

"Me too." The mother agreed

"But that's not the same as losing a villa."

"Well, the sea did part of that."

"How?"

"It spent years crashing against the cliffs the villa was sitting on, eroding the rocks beneath it, breaking the walls apart."

"But you said there was more to the villa."

"Did I? Well, there might be, I suppose."

"How can you suppose it but not know it?"

"Well, we can't know what isn't discovered, can we?"

"So, there's still some villa to discover?" Rhys asked.

"It's possible."

"But it might be impossible." Lyra asked.

"It might. But you see, before they found the villa crumbling from the cliffs, they found a part of a Roman bath house further inland."

"How much further?"

"Not much, somewhere near the hotels. They said there was a long corridor leading to it from the crumbling villa."

"What happened to that then?"

"Can we see it?"

"Well no, it was left exposed for people to see and tourists came and took bits of it away with them."

"Why did they do that?"

"Like a souvenir I suppose – to remember their day by the sea – or to remember the Romans or to hold a bit of history. You like to collect old things, don't you?"

"Yes, bits of tile and pot and things." Lyra said.

"I like collecting stones and fossils." Rhys said.

"Yes well, a bit like that. Having old things makes you think about where they've come from and who made them and who used them and that sort of thing."

"So, there's no bath house?"

"No."

"And no long corridor."

"No, well maybe."

"And no villa."

"No."

"What is there then?"

"Two tiles."

"Huh."

"They're big tiles – for a Roman heating system. They're kind of fancy."

"Did you say people wrote about it?"

"Oh, yes, a few people actually."

"And they said they saw it?"

"They did."

"Can we read what they wrote?"

"Yes, we can."

"And someone drew it?"

"Yes, someone did. They're pretty good drawings actually. They show the walls of some of the rooms and a corridor. You can see how close the villa was to the cliff edge."

"Why did they build it there?"

"Hmm?"

"So close to the cliff edge?"

"Oh, well there was more land back then."

"What happened to the land?"

"The sea claimed it."

They could see the sea in the distance, waves silvered by streetlights and a low white moon.

"Why didn't they take photos?"

"Yeah, you can trust a photo."

"This was before cameras."

"How long ago was it?"

"Was what?"

"That they found it."

"Oh, people found it three hundred years ago, and two hundred years ago, then a hundred years ago... more of it just kept turning up."

"A hundred years ago isn't before cameras."

"No, but they didn't take photos."

"They could have."

"They should have."

"Is someone going to find some more now?"

"Why do you think that?"

"Well, if they find it every hundred years?"

"Someone did look recently."

"They did?"

"Yes."

"Where?"

"Under the Carpet Gardens, by the pier."

"Did they find it?"

"Not really. Though they found a place where some of the greensand blocks had been removed."

"Huh."

"That could have been a Roman quarry."

"Huh."

"They found some Roman pottery."

"What like a bowl?"

"Or a plate?"

"No, just bits of pottery."

"Can we see them?"

"Perhaps."

"Can we go home now?"

"Sure. Shall we go the long way down by the road or through the woods?"

"Through the woods!"

"Ok. Look, there's a star – or is it a planet?"

"It's Mars!"

"Well, now that's a coincidence."

"Is it?"

"Mars was a Roman God – the God of War."

"Huh."

"Have you got your torches?"

"Yes."

LOOKING THROUGH DRAWINGS FROM THE VILLA ARCHIVE:

"I can see all the walls!"

"Look, they're really deep."

"What are they made of?"

"Sandstone, flint and mortar. The sandstone was green and quarried near the villa – like the stones used to build the walls around Pevensey Castle."

"Was it stone all the way up?"

"Oh no, it would have been made of bricks that were plastered over and giant timber beams to support the roof."

"Was it thatch?"

"No - tiles. The local people who didn't live in villas would have had round houses with thatched roofs."

"Where did they live?"

"Some of them had a settlement up on the Downs, near Beachy Head."

"Cool."

"I bet they hated each other."

"Why do you think that?"

"I would have done if I was a Briton, and the Romans came and took over."

"Yeah, and me. Did they have swords?"

"Who?"

"The Britons and the Romans."

"They both had swords, yes. But they didn't really stay Britons and Romans, they sort of became Romano-British."

"What does that mean?"

"It means that after a while, the Romans who settled here became more British and the British who lived here became more Roman."

"Huh."

"Can you see anything else in the pictures?"

"There's the corridor!"

"Did that lead to the bath house?"

"It's possible."

"I can see the Downs!"

"And a church in the back!"

"Yes, that's Trinity Church."

"Is it still there?"

"Yes."

"Where's that wall?"

"And those houses?"

"Not there anymore."

"Well, it doesn't look much like a villa." Lyra said.

"No. it doesn't look much like anything." Rhys said.

"I couldn't live in it."

"I wouldn't! And I wouldn't have been Romano-British."

"No?"

"No, I'd have been Britisho-Roman."

"Oh."

"Would I have had a sword?"

"It's possible."

"It's a funny story."

"Yeah, like a puzzle you can't finish."

"You're right, but I think it's an important story."

"Do you?"

"Why?"

"Because it means that our little town was part of the Roman Empire."

"It was?"

"Sure."

"That's cool."

"Yeah."

"Well you've seen some of the pictures of the villa and read some of the articles - What do you think?"

"I think they found a villa."

"Yeah, me too."

"So do I."

"Shame it's not there anymore." Lyra said.

"Well, it might be." The mother said.

"I think there's not much left." Rhys said.

"Yeah, just two tiles!"

"And maybe a statue."

"I'm not sure that counts."

"Me either."

"But there could still be some of the building there."

"Yeah, under the roads or hotels."

"It's possible."

"So, someone could find it one day."

"That would be good, wouldn't it?"

"Yeah!"

"Yeah!"

"So how does it feel to know there was a Roman villa in our town?"

"Awesome."

"Yeah, awesome."

"But it's still kind of, you know..."

"...Missing?"

"Yeah."

A FEW DAYS LATER:

"I've arranged a trip for you."

"To the ice cream parlour?" Lyra looked delighted.

"The cinema?" Rhys looked eager.

"No. A Roman villa."

"Oh, ok." Their faces dropped a little.

"Is it better than our one?" Rhys asked.

"Yes, much better. Well perhaps not better, just more – you know – still there."

"Are there mosaics?" Lyra asked.

"Yes, lots of them!"

"And a bathhouse?"

"Yes."

"A long corridor?"

"Yes."

"I bet there are tiles!"

"There are plenty of tiles, yes – and a hypocaust."

"I know about them!"

"Me too! They're for under-floor fires to heat the floors up!"

"Yes they are – well, the fires weren't exactly under the floors, because that would have led to.."

"Fire!"

"Yes, it was the hot air from the fires that circulated beneath the floors."

"I know that!"

"I know that too!"

"Yes, I thought you might. Right, well we're going to see something else as well – an actual Roman villa that you can walk into."

42

"No way!"

"Yes way, but it's not that old."

"How old?"

"Twenty years or so."

"That's not Roman then, is it? It's not old enough!"

"Ah, you got me, it's a reconstruction."

"Huh?"

"It's been built to look like a Roman villa – made out of the same sorts of materials a villa would have been made of."

"Tiles?"

"Yes, tiles! And timber and bricks and plaster.."

"Are there mosaics?"

"Yes, there's a mosaic!"

"Cool!"

"Yeah, cool!"

"You're going to come then? You wouldn't rather go for an ice cream?"

"What? No!" Rhys looked shocked.

"Can we have ice cream as well?" Lyra looked appealingly at her mother.

"Uh, maybe."

ON THE A27 JUST PAST CHICHESTER:

"Watch out for signs to Fishbourne!"

"Fish born? Ugh, what's that?"

"Fishbourne – it's where we're going to find a villa."

"And where fish are born?"

"No! F-I-S-H-B-O-U-R-N-E."

"Why's it called that?"

"Beats me."

"I'll find the sign first!"

"No, I will!"

"No, I will.."

"Settle down, we'll all look out for it."

"There it is! I found it first!"

"No you didn't, I saw it too!"

"Yeah, but I was first!"

"No, I was!"

"We've driven straight past it!"

"Oh dear, we'll turn around."

"There's the sign!"

"It says Fishbourne Roman villa! There's a helmet on it!"

"Yes, we're nearly there."

"But it's all houses."

"And a school – is that a school? Imagine living right by a Roman villa!"

"Yeah, that'd be cool."

"Yeah."

IN THE EXHIBITION HALL AT FISHBOURNE ROMAN VILLA:

"Wow, it's big in here."

"Yeah, doesn't look much like a villa."

"No, it's the remains of one, you'll have to imagine how it looked."

"Again? We had to do that already!"

"Yeah, with the Eastbourne one."

"Yeah."

"Yes, well archaeology takes quite a bit of imagination."

"Does it?"

"Why?"

"Because most of the time there's nothing whole left, it's the remains of what there used to be, of what people made and used and left behind. It's not a complete story, it's clues about the past."

"Huh."

"So, it's all made up?"

"No, not all of it. There are some things we can know for certain."

"Like what?"

"Like – these people lived many years before us and they learned how to build big, beautiful houses and they learned how to craft beautiful objects and established trade routes around the world to bring in foods and products from many different places. We know that they were influenced by the ancient Greeks and that their influence still carries on in our society."

"It does?"

"How do we know that?"

"Yes – we know from the archaeological record – indoor toilets? Roman. Indoor wall paintings? Roman. Tiled houses.."

"Not tiles again!"

"I know what you're going to say…"

"Yes?"

"Romans gave us tiled houses."

"They did!"

"So, what they did… how many thousand years ago?"

"Let's say two."

"…What they did two thousand years ago still affects us?"

"Yes. Can you think of anything else that's still quite Roman-inspired?"

"Roads. Straight ones."

"Mosaics."

"Good. Where do we find mosaics?"

"I've seen them at the bottom of the swimming pool."

"In our bathroom!"

"Well, that gives me another idea. Where did we get the idea of bathrooms?"

"THE ROMANS!" chorused two excited children.

"Yup."

"What else, what else?"

"The letters we use, the language we speak."

"Hey, I don't speak Latin!" Lyra looked indignant.

"I do! Puella! Puer!" Rhys grinned.

"You're just swearing."

"Am not!"

"Yes, those are Latin words, but the alphabet we use is Latin and we have common words we say all the time that the Romans gave us."

"We do?"

"Huh."

"Alpha; versus; percent…"

"Not maths!"

"I love maths!"

"What's all that got to do with a villa?"

"Good question. It's about the people who built and lived in the villas –

they changed the society so much that their influence still exists all these years later."

"Oh."

"What's there to see here then?"

"You show me..."

ABOVE THE MOSAICS:

"WOW!"

"WOW!"

"Yep, wow!"

"Is that cupid?"

"It looks like myths!"

"Yeah."

"Look at that creature!"

"I know about it! It's a sea horse but they didn't know what that was, so they gave a horse a fishy tail!" Rhys pointed to the picture on the villa floor.

"Yeah, and that one's a sealion but it's a lion with a tail!" Lyra laughed.

"That's funny!"

"Yeah!"

"And look at that dolphin! Have you ever seen a tail like it!"

"It's too long!"

"And there's an angel riding it!"

"Maybe Cupid?"

They followed the boardwalks around the Hall.

"See that low wall there? It's where the walls of the villa would have been."

"I can imagine it!"

"I can too!"

"Yes?"

"Yeah – and there are paintings all-round the walls!"

"And sofas!"

"Yeah, and there are slaves walking around with food."

"Yeah, and Romans relaxing."

"Yes? You can imagine all that?"

"YEAH!" The children grinned.

LEAVING THE CAFÉ:

"I'm going to lick my ice-cream really slowly."

"Yeah, I'll see how long mine lasts."

"Mine will last longer..."

"We've got plenty of time until we get to the next place, take all the time you need."

"How long?"

"About half an hour."

ARRIVING AT BUTSER ANCIENT FARM:

"Here we are."

"I'm tired"

"I know, it's been a long drive and a lot to take in."

"I liked those mosaics!"

"I liked them!"

"I know, me too. You ready?"

"Yes!"

"It's this way, look!"

"I want to feed the goats!"

"Ok, we'll do that first."

"Ooh, her tongue's so tickly."

"I don't want to feed her."

"Me either."

"Ok, hand it over. Oh, it is tickly!"

"Yeah."

"Let's wash our hands and.,."

"Find a villa!"

"I want to see an Iron Age house!"

"Yeah, and me, and I want to see that Stone Age one…"

"And the Saxon one…"

"We can see them all!"

OUTSIDE THE ROMAN VILLA RECONSTRUCTION:

"Well, what's it like?"

"It's big and posh."

"Yes? What else do you think?"

"It's not as big as our one."

"The Eastbourne one? No, I suppose not."

"I like the white walls."

"And the red stripe."

"Look at all those tiles!"

"I told you there'd be tiles!"

"Shall we go in?"

"It's like being in Ancient Rome!"

"Is it?"

"Yes, we're all Romans and this is our house, and we live in Eastbourne and if we open that front door, we'll see the sea and…"

"And I've got my own room and I go to school…"

"You don't, you're a girl!"

"I do, I wouldn't let you go without me!"

"You couldn't choose!"

"I could!"

"Alright, what can you notice in here that's like what we've been discussing?"

"Wall paintings! I like that one, it looks like picture frames."

"Yeah, without pictures in it."

"Look at that mosaic!"

"It's not as good as Fishbourne."

"What does that tell you?"

"That they weren't as rich?"

"Okay."

"Yeah, they weren't as high status."

"That's a Roman word! Where did you read it?"

"At the exhibition."

"Oh."

"What's this?"

"A shrine to the household gods."

"That's funny."

"What's this room?"

"Looks like a kitchen."

"Look at all those spices!"

"I like the windows."

"Yeah."

"Look, there's a toilet!"

"Yes!"

"OK, what are we learning?"

"That being Roman's fun!"

"Yes?"

"They had a lot of cool stuff."

"And they lived in bright houses."

"What do you think the native Britons would have thought of them?"

"Villas or Romans?"

"Both."

"They would have thought they were weird." Lyra wrinkled up her nose.

"Yeah, and that they were show-offs." Rhys acted out a showing-off walk.

"And they would have been jealous of them."

"Do you think so?"

"Yes. They only had mud and sticks to build with."

"Shall we go and look at an Iron Age house?"

"Okay."

"Sure."

INSIDE A RECONSTRUCTED IRON AGE ROUNDHOUSE:

"It's beautiful!"

"I like how the fire warms the whole room."

"It's cosy."

"Yeah. I'd sleep here."

"I'd be over this side."

"It smells really nice!"

"Smoky!"

"Look at the loom, we'd be making our own clothes on that."

They ran their fingers over the wooden frame.

"Is it better than a Roman villa?"

"Not better, I think."

"Nah, it's darker."

"And there's only one room – nowhere to go."

"Does it feel like we're in a house of mud and sticks?"

"Nah, it's pretty cool."

"Yeah. Way better than I thought."

"Would you like to be Britisho-Roman living in here then? Or Romano-British living in a villa?"

"I'd live in a villa."

"Yeah, me too."

"But I'd have this as a holiday home."

"Yeah, it's like camping!"

A WEEK LATER, BY THE CARPET GARDENS:

"What can you remember?"

"I remember that the Roman villa was here – under the road!"

"Yeah, and it had a long corridor."

"…and red tiles!"

"Yeah, lots of tiles, and high white walls!"

"Why do you think they were white?"

"The house we went into was white."

"Yeah."

"Okay, anything else?"

"There were lots of rooms."

"And a hypocaust!"

"And a kitchen, and bedrooms, and there would have been mosaics!"

"Yeah, sealions and seahorses!"

"I bet they had seagirls instead of seagulls!"

"Yeah, like mermaids!"

"Maybe."

"And there was a bath house they could walk to, to have a swim!"

"Yeah, with tiles all round it!"

"What if we could see the walls here, like we saw walls at Fishbourne?"

"Well, we'd be able to picture all the people walking around inside the villa then."

"Yes?"

"Yeah – and we could picture all the furniture too!"

"What do you think that would be like?"

"It would be like we could bring history to life."

"Yeah, it would feel more real, like it actually happened here."

"That's a good idea."

"And if it was like the other one – the Butser one…"

"Haha!"

"Butt!"

"Butt!"

"Hahaha!"

"We could walk in it."

"I'd open the door here and step right in."

"It would be cool in there, and a little dark, but there would be windows."

"Yeah, and the corridor would be wide and long, and we could run up it."

"Yeah, we'd be running on mosaics."

"And eating grapes."

"I like grapes."

"Me too."

"And what about the rest of the town, what would they be doing while you were being like the Romans?"

"Oh, that's easy. They'd be cooking their food on a fire in a big roundhouse."

"Yeah, and sharpening their swords to come and get rid of the Romans!"

"They could have been local people with wealth, remember? Maybe not Roman at all."

"Oh yeah."

"They can't have hated each other for long."

"Why?"

"Yeah why?"

"Well, they stopped fighting eventually, didn't they, when they stopped calling themselves Britons or Romans and they just became neighbours."

"Huh."

"I suppose the Saxons weren't all Saxon then?"

"I suppose not!"

"But they fought the Romans…"

"Romano-British – yes."

"Britisho…"

"…Yes, we know!"

"It's complicated, isn't it?"

"It is. Shall we go home now?"

"Yes! Can we get an ice cream first?"

"We'll see…"

Pestilence in Thrall
November 664CE

An Anglo-Saxon cemetery was discovered on Ocklynge Hill in March 1970. The Saxons buried there had very few grave goods with them, just the occasional iron knife. Scientific testing of the human remains indicated that they had been buried around 650 to 770CE.

Some three quarters of a mile away, another Anglo-Saxon cemetery was discovered, between 1991 and 1992, at the top of St. Anne's Road. Sixty-nine inhumation burials and five cremation burials were archaeologically investigated, these burials contained many rich grave goods, which had been left with the dead for use in the afterlife. Personal items including tweezers and ear scoops, golden jewellery and fashion items, keys, and bags of beads, lay interred along with swords, shields and spears, and exquisite glass vessels. Scientific dating evidence from this cemetery showed that the burials were mostly earlier in date, from 420 to 550CE, but there were also a few later ones ranging from 650 to 750CE.

A religious conversion driven by the increasingly powerful church of Rome caused a shift from Paganism to Christianity during the late sixth and early seventh centuries. It is very likely that the St. Anne's Road cemetery was a Pagan-Saxon burial ground while the Ocklynge Hill cemetery was a Christian-Saxon burial ground. There was a brief period of time where both graveyards were in use.

This story of a Welsh slave-girl and her Saxon owners explores the divide between old and new beliefs and the chilling consequences of an invisible danger from across the sea.

Anglo-Saxon Glossary

Blod-monath (Blood-month, November)

Cofgodas (Household Gods)

Ealdwulf (Old wolf)

Fríge (Anglo-Saxon goddess, wife of Wöden)

Hlaford (Lord)

Mercian (from Mercia, middle England)

Modor (Mother)

Mónagifu (gift from the moon)

Modraniht (Mother Night, Winter Solstice)

Sigel (rune/the sun)

Suth Seaxa (South Saxons)

Theow (a bonded slave)

Thunor (Anglo-Saxon god of thunder)

Tiw (Anglo-Saxon god of war)

Wealh (foreign/welsh)

Wif (Wife)

Wöden (Anglo-Saxon All-Father god)

Wöden's daeg (Woden's day/Wednesday)

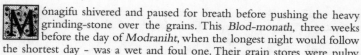

ónagifu shivered and paused for breath before pushing the heavy grinding-stone over the grains. This *Blod-monath*, three weeks before the day of *Modraniht*, when the longest night would follow the shortest day – was a wet and foul one. Their grain stores were pulpy, edged with pools of water and nibbled at by drenched rats. What was left was tainted and sour, left a taste in the mouth that couldn't be disturbed by fish or leaf. The villager's pigs were slaughtered, save for the favoured one, who was getting skinnier by the day. Her mistress's children coddled the pig, saved it scraps from their plates and bones from the cooking pot. The favoured pig's mother and siblings had been blooded the week before and now hung from the rafters of the smoking-house. Mónagifu warned her charges, Aebbe and Osbeorn, not to name the pig, not to favour it, for it would surely not last the winter, but who would listen to a *theow*?

Mónagifu had been born a free Briton, from the county of Gwynedd, the tongue of her mother had been Welsh, or *foreign-wealh* as her Saxon owners called her. She'd been raised on the peninsula of Ll n on the Irish Sea. Sand and tall grasses and fishing nets dogged her fading memories of home – *a blazing fire in the hearth and her mother's lamb cawl bubbling; her father's tales of magic and war; them all spinning wool and weaving tales through the long dark winters.* Her father had told her stories, borrowed from the bards, of whole forests of magic trees that had ripped their roots out of the earth to march overland and join the fight against the Saxons. The whole of Wales, she knew, had battled against invasion and conversion, even the land and all her bounty. Her mother had been soft-eyed and warm, her father broad, dark, and quick to anger, quick to laughter. He'd died in battle against the Mercian Saxons. Soon after, her mother had been pulled from their home by strangers' hands and she (*Mona* then, for the moon) had been plucked from her chair and brought here, to the land of the South Saxons, nearer the land of the Franks than Ireland. She'd been sick for her mam and her home ever since.

They said they'd free her to marry when the time came, her master *Hlaford* Ealdwulf and his *wif* Aethelflaed had promised. Could she trust the word of a *Saxon*? Mónagifu wasn't sure. Her friend Mildgyd, Aethelflaed's first *theow*, had found neither love nor freedom since being bound to the *Hlaford's* wif – and Mildgyd had ten years on Mónagifu.

Hlaford Ealdwulf, the village chief, was the keeper-of-legends – not like the epic poems of King Arthur that Taliesin had sung to the Welsh princes – but tales of war and giants, of *Beowulf* the Brave, *Hrothgar* the Crazed, and the Nine Herbs of *Wöden*; of wildmen-devourers and dragons; dwarves and elven-folk. Aethelflaed often told him to throw those old stories away, to tell the stories of the one-god and his suffering son instead, but Ealdwulf said he'd leave those stories to the monks.

The monks came often from over-the-seas with crosses of wood and metal and pages of symbols, like the Romans used, not the Saxon runes Mónagifu saw burned into shields and etched into door lintels and the shrines-of-the dead. The monk's symbols covered pages and pages of bound, dried tree-pulp and they treated them like gold. The monks came from Rome - where the one-god stories came from – and from all over Italy, from the many lands of the Franks, and from Ireland. They brought tales of paradise and fiery-hell and pestilence that ravaged whole cities. Mónagifu, a good listener, thought their tales dull and morbid and would often find herself imagining her homespun tales or Ealdwulf's stories even while the monks were talking. She couldn't understand Aethelflaed's love for the monks or her insistence that the villagers love the Roman religion. Mónagifu's own mother had secretly cherished Druid lore over Christian worship, and Mónagifu thought she was very much like her mother.

"Mónagifu, Mónagifu! Osbeorn has fled to find the men at the shore. He says spinning is women's work and he's no woman, he's a fisherman. Stop him running off, Mónagifu. Tell him." Aebbe pleaded, her clear blue eyes brimming with tears.

"Now Aebbe, you can see I'm busy. Where's your *modor*? She can help with Osbeorn."

"She's too tired, Mónagifu. She didn't get up today."

"Didn't get up again? So, I have the spinning to do as well, do I? Tch."

"But what about Osbeorn?"

"Oh Aebbe, take Mildgyd with you and find Osbeorn and tell him that if he doesn't return home that the *cofgodas* will come in the night and steal his spear and shield and the elves will sour all his food." Aebbe's eyes grew wide. "Not really, Aebbe. You just tell him that to fright him and get him to come back." Aebbe grinned warily, coughed, and ran off after her brother.

Mónagifu stood carefully, aches deep in her back and coursing through her fingers. Grinding the grains was the hardest labour in the village and none but *theows* ground their bones away over the grinding-stone, not the freemen or men-of-status - they broke their bones in battle. Mónagifu's body felt old, like she wore the skin and bones of an elder.

Ealdwulf's settlement of long-houses, sunken-huts and barns hugged the side of a chalky hill, between the salty sea that separated the Seaxa-land and Frank-land, and the dragon's mound that curved round the Burne valley – a huge beast that slumbered over the settlements. The dragon's mound was older than time, the elders said, even the ancient Britons who'd built their tombs and sacred mounds upon its back had no connection with its beginning. One of the ancients' mounds stood near their settlement - a rounded earthen hillock bounded by a circular ditch - but that was the relic of a heathen-past. The future, their king told them, was Christian, not Pagan. Hadn't they learned that after the Battle of *Winwaed*? Hadn't they known that when he – Aethelwalh – had pledged his loyalty to the one-god and married a Christian bride? His people, all the South Saxons, must follow his lead, he said. Aethelflaed nodded, yes, oh yes, while the others silently groaned and left offerings for the hidden-folk.

Mónagifu remembered the Battle of the *Winwaed*, for it had taken her father, her mother, and her freedom. "The death of the Pagan!" they'd cried from the bloody battlefield as the river Winwaed ran red with pagan blood. Aethelflaed had ensured that she heard the bloody tale over and over, as Mónagifu grew from a tiny, frightened stolen child to a resigned, grown *theow*. But she never stopped searching for another side to the story, one that named her father a hero for fighting in battle with his Welsh kin and the Pagan King Penda of Mercia, against Oswiu, Christian King of Northumbria. They lost, the Pagans, but at least they had resisted conversion. It was something, Mónagifu knew, to fight for the old stories.

The elders remembered a time when the ancient-mound had been the centre of their own burial-ground, the elder's elders had told of the tales their elders had told them, of the first settlers from Saxony, who'd brought their rich culture and fine treasures with them, and who sent their belongings with their dead to the afterlife. Legends told of ancestral graves filled with gold and jewels and all the riches of Saxony. Now the gold of the *eald Seaxe* – the old Saxons - lay below ground with the bones of the ancient Britons, side by side on the sacred hill. The Saxons had claimed this territory as their own, once the Romans and Britons had been purged from it – this fertile valley, its chalky cliffs and rocky shore – now they belonged to the land as much as any tribe who'd dwelt there before them.

Aethelflaed had told her that they did not perform the gold-burials anymore, because the true god didn't need grave-gifts. She said it was heathen to think that men needed gold and food in the afterlife, and her god would welcome all, even those without wealth and status. For Aethelflaed, a warrior's grave was something from the legends of *Wöden, Fríge, Thunor,* and *Tiw,* old-gods, and that was all in the past. Stories for children and old men.

Mónagifu shivered and wiped her hand across her brow. She felt hot and clammy, her eyes heavy in their sockets. So Aethelflaed was staying abed today? Mónagifu felt ire rise in her gorge, they'd all got enough work to do to keep the village fed and clothed for the winter. Did Aethelflaed really think she could leave it to the *theows* and *common-wifs*? She made her way to Ealdwulf's Hall, past the spinning huts and grain stores, past the favoured pig and pecking hens, the oyster and mussel baths and salted fish stores.

"Aethelflaed?" she called. "Aethelflaed?" Silence greeted her. "Aethelflaed, are you there? Osbeorn has run away. Aethelflaed?" Was that a moan she heard? Or a chill wind in the rafters?

"Are you there, Aethelflaed?" This time, the moan was unmistakeable, no wind had ever sounded so bleak. Mónagifu pulled the bed-curtain aside. "Aethelflae..?" Aethelflaed was indeed abed, lying on top of the covers, her skin glistening with wet heat. The smell of her was rancid and her face was too vile to look at - her nose blackened and skin yellowed, her eyes sunken and blood-shot, her hair wet and lank against hollow-cheeks.

Mónagifu swore and spat behind her, averting the curse from her own skin. Aethelflaed tried to sit up but her limbs were weak and wouldn't hold her. Her words died on cracked lips as she writhed horribly; her bed-clothes rose to reveal black lumps protruding from her thighs. As she watched, Aethelflaed's head fell forward and she vomited, a stream of bloody-liquid like the pagan-river of her tales. Mónagifu backed away, calling for help, running, running until her legs gave way and she fell to the floor, sobbing. *What curse this? What curse this?* Aethelflaed-the-Holy – Aethelflaed-the-Righteous – Aethelflaed-the-Dying. Ah! Was this Justinian's curse - the unholy pestilence the monks had warned of? Surely it had not been sent for Aethelflaed.

The children! Mónagifu stumbled down the hillside, dipped her hand in the waters of the Burne and wiped her hot face and neck, she stumbled on through field and meadow to the shore. Ealdwulf was there, with his nets and fishing-traps, home from the fishing-trip at last, the men of the village were wading through the icy water to haul their meagre catch to the sand. Aebbe was by Ealdwulf's side, Mildgyd behind them, looking at her in confusion. Mónagifu called out. "Ealdwulf! Ealdwulf!" Her call was a scream, sprung from a well-of-fear. He turned, startled, annoyed, and returned his gaze to the sea. "Ealdwulf!" Mónagifu repeated. "Ealdwulf! It's Aethelflaed.."

"What's that you say? Why aren't you at your work? Have you let Osbeorn stray? Aebbe says you wouldn't help her, you should remember your place, *theow*."

Mónagifu stumbled forward, looking Ealdwulf directly in the eye, panting with the heat of the run, the breathlessness of fright. "Aethelflaed.. the curse..." She slowed her breath and tried again, her words ragged. "..Just.. Justinian's pestilence.."

Ealdwulf crossed himself with his fingers and spat behind him.

Mónagifu looked Aebbe all-over. *Was she tired-looking - was her skin yellowed, her eyes shadowed?* Aebbe coughed as Mónagifu watched, her father patted her back and drew her nearer.

"Aethelflaed's sick with the buboes, Ealdwulf.." Mónagifu looked at Aebbe, swallowed hard, loath to name the truth in front of her. "..Dying."

Aebbe let out a sob. "No." Ealdwulf shook his head. "Mildgyd when did you last see Aethelflaed? Go to her now and tell her to come, prove this wretch wrong."

"I.." Mildgyd looked scared. "Aethelflaed wanted to be left alone, she.. she said she wasn't feeling herself and wanted to be alone.. she…" Ealdwulf slapped her, a great red weal rose upon her cheek.

"When?"

"Yesterday, first thing, she wasn't hungry for her food, she sent me away."

"How was she then? How did she look?"

"I.. I didn't see her clearly, it was early, the house was in shadow."

Ealdwulf cursed. He looked at Mónagifu, "You lie."

"No, I do not lie. You shall know it." Mónagifu held her arms open for Aebbe, who ran into them, still sobbing. "There, there, *cariad*, there, there." She stroked Aebbe's hair, shivering at the memory of Aethelflaed. Shivering too, at the touch of Aebbe's clammy skin.

Osbeorn wasn't found for another two days. He'd fallen in the woods and twisted his ankle, by the time they found him, his face and hands had blackened and hard black lumps had grown across his little body. They carried him, limp and weak back to the village and laid him next to his mother, who hadn't opened her eyes since Mónagifu had first found her. Aethelflaed was unrecognisable now, her face as black as night, the stench of death upon her, even as she pulled shallow breaths from the air.

Aebbe, pretty-little Aebbe, sobbed for her mother and brother but shed no tear for herself, even as her fingers and toes dried and blackened, and her skin throbbed with pain. She lay in Mónagifu's arms as the life flew from her on a shaky breath.

Mónagifu, tenderly closed Aebbe's pale blue eyes and carried her to her mother's side. All three of them, blackened and stricken by the pestilence, and many of the villagers sick and ailing. Who should they pray to - they begged each other for the answer - who would listen? The old gods betrayed, the one-god piqued, who would help them now? They left morsels for the hob-fairies, sacrificed the favoured pig, called for their Mother-the-Earth to protect them, but the pestilence was swift and merciless.

They buried Aethelflaed and her children, side by side, in the new burial-ground over the hill. No jewels to pay their way, no sword or spear to reflect their valiant natures, no food to sustain them on their journey, just Aethelflaed's faith in redemption.

Mónagifu begged not to be taken there when her time came, which she knew would be soon. "Please." She said, "Not there." They called for Ealdwulf as she lay in the straw, weak and mumbling. He came and pitied what he saw. He listened to her wishes and remembered Aebbe and the care she had been shown.

Mónagifu died on a *Wöden's daeg,* a moon-or-so before the start of her nineteenth year. True to his word, Ealdwulf laid her down in the old grounds, near the ancient mound, and even sent her away with a meal for her journey, a loaf of bread dipped in mead, a *sigel* for the sun etched into the crust. For Ealdwulf knew that the moon must follow the sun on its journey through the heavens, no matter which god ruled the sky.

Sanctuary
1248CE

t. Mary's Church in Old Town is the oldest church in Eastbourne, it was built at the turn of the thirteenth century and greatly altered a century later. The church served as an important Chapel for the Treasurer of Chichester Cathedral, and as a rather grandiose Parish Church from the 1240's onwards. It was the hub of village life and the focal point for births, marriages, and burials, and all the festivities in between. Over eight hundred years of Eastbourne history and the lives of countless townsfolk have been played out within its vaulted walls. The church was a place of sanctuary, where people could claim respite from their troubles on the outside. The early medieval concept of crime and punishment was severe and intolerant, its sole purpose to dissuade crime and criminality. The criminally minded greatly feared exile, or abjuration from the realm. Those wrong doers who were sent into exile were never permitted back into the country, yet some preferred that to the old-fashioned alternatives.

This story concerns two divergent brothers, their loyalty to each other and their community, their flight into sanctuary, and their dealings with the law.

stumble over a low wall and fall to the ground, my knees banging hard on frozen earth. A thin moon shines faintly in the darkness, its light too feeble to guide my path.

"Get on your feet!" Thomas hisses. "Run!" He grabs my shoulder and heaves me upwards, pulling me along behind him. A bell is clanging behind us, we can hear footsteps following our trail through the night. They've raised the hue and cry and we're fast, but one of them has a lamp, with light to guide them they'll be faster still. Running again, my feet a wisp behind Thomas', an icy wind numbs my cheeks and nose. I slam hard into cold stone and curse, my fingers, feeling for the obstacle, run over letters: words I've never learned, spongey moss, creeping lichen. "Hurry brother."

I imagine the words I would yell at Thomas if my tongue wasn't stuck behind my teeth, which are clenched in shivering fury. None of them are pretty. He's done it again, he's done it again, I think as he pulls me towards a great, dark doorway. He's led me through darkness our whole lives, never content with an honest living, never content at all, always restless, driven by avarice and self-pity. He disgusts me, he is my shame and our whole tithing's shame. Our disgrace and our punishment on this earth.

"John! Stop there! Thomas!" They're closer still, their cries reverberate round the graveyard. My brother firms his grip on my sleeve. I hear the seam rip and I want to scream. The threshold ahead of us is a line I should not cross; once inside, I'm as guilty as Thomas. If I'm not already.

"John, come back to us. For shame! Don't go with him." I feel Hugh's hot breath on the air behind me, his lamp burning just behind my back, casting shadows before me, illuminating Thomas' retreating figure, and the caen-stone arch ahead with the great-oak door ajar. I'd know Hugh's voice anywhere, we've been tithe-brothers these twenty years, boys-in-mock-armour before that, playing sword-games with sticks and shields of bark. He's angry, his breath seething. I don't turn to face him; I don't even stop running. Like a marionette pulled by Thomas' fingers, I follow him inside the church.

"Sanctuary!" Thomas shouts as he steps inside. "Sanctuary. We claim sanctuary!"

"Who goes there?" A voice, stern, and solid calls from the cold darkness. Robert de Boseham appears from the chancel, a candle thrust forward in front of him as he peers through the gloom at us.

"It is I, Thomas Skinner and my brother, John Weaver," Thomas answers boldly. "We claim sanctuary."

I stand there as if dreaming, my breath pluming out in great white coils of smoke, my chest heaving. I can't meet the Rector's eyes and I daren't look at Thomas. I stare instead at a carved stone-face on the nave column in front of me, its haunted eyes and downturned mouth glare out at the night we've just left behind.

"Toss them back out, Father!" Gilbert has pushed his way past Hugh and is approaching us down the southern aisle. "We'll see that justice is done." He's leering, as is his wont. Gilbert's another like Thomas who won't settle in peace. He's due at the King's Assizes any day now, in answer for the mysterious death of Remigius de Esthalle, found five nights ago drowned in the sea. Not that many are weeping for Remigius' loss, but if Gilbert is guilty of any part in his death, we'll all pay for it. Our tithing bears the burden of every man in it. I won't be surprised if they rule for suicide though, Remigius always had lived on the bitter edge of life. Now this, now Thomas. I pray this will end well but I don't see how it can.

"Sanctuary has been called, Gilbert atte Welle. It is not your place to administer justice. I will hear these men announce their deeds and you will remain outside. Call for the sheriff if you must be present." Rector Robert stands tall, an imposing stature, even night-shrouded.

Gilbert laughs at Robert and lunges for Thomas, grabbing him by the collar and pinning him to the nearest column. His face is as close to Thomas' as he can get it, his eyes pinched with hatred. "I will see you hung for this, Thomas Skinner, so help me god." He punches Thomas in the stomach, so he folds over, and then spits on his face.

"Enough, Gilbert." Robert commands.

Gilbert kicks Thomas to the floor as he turns to leave, returning for another punch, and another. I know how he feels. Thomas is sitting there on the floor, blood on his teeth and trickling down his nose and he's grinning.

"Enough, I say!" Robert de Boseham has established himself between Gilbert and Thomas. I have done nothing.

Robert helps Thomas to his feet and leads him to the back of the church. We used to sit there as children, with our own father who'd watched the nave built from the ground-up with all that fine, pale building stone from Normandy. There was an Abbey over there in France, he told us, that owned our church and all its lands. They sent their own stone over to make sure the new church was built right, in honour of God and King. Our father was honouring them in his own way, pushing up the wild-orchids in the graveyard.

"Are you with us, John?" Hugh and Little Walter are reaching for Gilbert, soothing him. I don't know, I just don't know. I shake my head. Hugh, still clutching the lamp is pleading with me. "John?"

"John!" Little Walter cries, his eyes shining in disbelief. "It'll go harder on us if the both of you stay. Whatever he's done, it can't have been your fault.

Come."

They're so insistent. They'll suffer for this, who knows what - fines they can't afford to pay - labour they can't afford to give - imprisonment that will break their families apart?

"Think of Elizabeth and the boys, John..."

Thomas catches my eye and beckons and I find myself walking down the church, away from the altar, away from my tithe-brothers. The door slams behind me and I carry on walking. Thomas is already confessing.

"I did walk into Richard de Yngeham's house, believing him to be away in London for the while, and did take from his chest a little trifle of a thing. He owed me you see, for a year's worth of furs and leather, and there's him richer than a man can be and travelling all over and me hungrier than a famine-mite. It was all I could do to survive these last weeks and a man's needs do catch up to him. It were a wrong thing, I know this Father, but I was in need and the church is here to help those in need, is that not so?"

"And you have the.. little trifle..?"

"Uh.." Thomas pats his cloak, feigning surprise. "..it must have dropped in the chase."

"I see. But what really brings you inside these doors this night?"

Thomas looks taken aback, as though the question were a surprise. The truth wars behind his expression with the deceit he so often prefers.

"I had been wrong about Richard's whereabouts. He had returned from his travels and discovered me in his chamber."

"..And?"

"..and he did attack me with his sword. He would have murdered me. All I did was in defence of myself and my brother."

They're both looking at me, I step forward, draw back my shoulders. My damned brother, born liar. Richard owed him nothing. I clear my throat, nearly choke on my own tongue. "We were walking home, Thomas was to stay with me until he could find work and lodgings." Thomas is glaring at me. "..He.. uh.. He stopped near Richard's house, told me he had a meeting with him, and I was to wait for their dealings to end before joining him by the tavern."

My cheeks are flaming with shame, my eyes roving over the carved arches and high glazed-windows, anywhere but the vicar's face. My words are true. Almost.

"You were with Thomas when this theft occurred?"

"I was but.."

"..and what occurred afterwards?"

I hang my head, squeeze my eyes to hold back the water that tries to flow from them. "Thomas came back with his sword bloody."

"Bloody, you say? What had been done?"

"I do not know." I say.

"And you did not stop to find out?"

"I.." my head is shaking of its own accord.

"Thomas Skinner. Tell me now, how fares Richard de Yngeham?"

Thomas is thinking over his reply, it is slow to come. "I believe Richard de Yngeham to be dead. It was through no fault of mine, but rather his own fault for withholding payment and attacking me."

Robert pales and his words catch in his throat. "Ach..." He pauses to catch his breath, "Then you are both in need of prayer, as are your tithing. You will be offered no leniency for this crime, not this time, Thomas Skinner. The sheriff will like as not order your hanging." Thomas swallows hard, his hands rising to his throat.

"Exile. I'll take exile." he cries.

Rector Robert nods, looks at me. "John? You'll claim exile with your brother?"

Exile? What would I do in France with no friends, no chattels, without Elizabeth and my boys - with Thomas? I'd be as good as dead, cast out of my own country with my brother at my back as a devil riding my shoulder. No.

"I'll put myself at the mercy of the country, Father." His eyes look worried before he nods and leads us to a bench. He takes out some blankets and offers them to us. I take one and wrap it round myself, try to curl up on the narrow wooden seat and squeeze my eyes closed. I hear Thomas shuffling along next to me, he's snoring before I have even finished a round of Hail Mary's. I feel the Rector's hand on my shoulder. "I'll pray for your better fortune, John Weaver." he says, before walking away to raise the sheriff from his slumber, his shoes ringing soundly on the stone floor. A distant door slams.

~

The days have passed in a blur. The Sheriff, on learning of my request for a hearing, let me return home. Thomas stayed at the church – his sanctuary – and the only safe place for him to stay. The tithing would have marched him to the court as soon as he stepped outside, dragged him to his death if they could. But he has claimed exile, so the gallows are not for him. Some part of me must need to protect him, as the church protects his body, his soul. As he slept on the cold, hard pews, I held my wife close, hugged my boys.

The court convened in the early days of January, in the 33rd year of the reign of our King Henry III, and I stood alone, waiting for the King's justice to decide on my fate. Real justice would have been being born without a brother.

~

Towns-people have gathered outside the church and down the road that leads to the edge of our villages, where the Burne stream gives way to meadow and marsh. I wonder if the whole Hundred has come for the spectacle of Exile. I see folk from Upperton and Mill Beverington, from Upwick and Chalvington, Lamport and Esthall. My tithing are at my back, champing like stabled horses waiting for a gallop. They'd charge Thomas down if they could, trample him into the earth. He's cost us a huge fine, we'll go hungry and practically destitute as we pay the debt back slowly, tied forever to the mess that Thomas has made of our lives. Hugh's hand is steady on my shoulder, his presence is stalwart, though the heat from his fingertips betrays his simmering rage. Gilbert has been cleared of the charges levelled against him, there were many who spoke of his good character and of Remigius' melancholic tendencies. Suicide they said, and Gilbert walks free. Gravestones surround the church, stone after stone standing tall above the bones of the departed. I send a silent greeting to father, to mother, then inwardly curse them for raising a man such as Thomas.

Richard de Pevensee, Queen Eleanor's Steward of Aquila and Bailiff of Burne is standing at the church door, with the King's coroner, flanked by the Hundred Jury. The sheriff stands rigidly, sword in hand and beside him, his men are holding a vast wooden cross upright. It looks like the scene from Calvary before the Christ was hung. No one doubts our Thomas's guilt though. Robert de Boseham leads Thomas from the church to the door, where his sanctuary will soon be ended, and his exile will begin.

"Repeat after me, Thomas Skinner of Lamport.." the Coroner states. "..'Hear this, O ye coroners, that I will go forth from this realm of England and hither I will not return..'.."

"I cannot say all that.." Thomas complains.

"..'save by leave of the lord King and his heirs, so help me God.'.."

"I tell you I cannot say all that, my tongue won't speak it."

The crowd jeers and nays at Thomas, ready to force the words from his felonious mouth. The sheriff steps forward and twists Thomas's arm behind him, leaning over his shoulder with threats pouring into his ear. Thomas looks full-frightened now. He knows he's escaped worse judgement, worse punishment than abjuration of the realm. He's only to look at me to confirm it. No one made him suffer trial-by-ordeal, no one put his crimes to the people of Sussex or the court of the King. For many, it looks as though

Thomas is escaping justice.

"Take the Oath, Thomas Skinner."

"I.. I.. will go forth..."

"From this Realm..."

"From this Realm..."

"Of England..."

He repeats the oath word-by-word, his face sullen, his eyes pinpricks of fright. A great cheer rises all around us as he finishes the pledge.

Thomas looks pitiful. His regular, well-cut raiments have been forfeit and in their stead, he wears a shapeless smock, carelessly stitched from shabby cloth. His feet are bare and already white with chill from the church's flagstone floor.

"You will make your way to Dover on foot, within three days hence, else you will be returned to Burne for swifter justice," the coroner intones. Thomas swallows, tries to catch my eye. I don't look at him.

In this cold season, with his bare skin exposed to frost and wind and rain, he'll be fortunate to make it to Dover with his life. They're making jest-and-jibe behind me, arguing over whether he'll survive one day or two; whether he'll try and flee before he arrives at the port; whether he'll drown on the boat-crossing over the channel or be attacked by hardened robbers in Wissant. No one believes he'll even survive a day in France without knowing a word of the language.

Elizabeth squeezes my hand, Hugh pats my shoulder, my boy John looks up at me with his eyes full of questions. I squeeze his hand and remain silent. This ordeal is torture to me, but I will see it through.

Richard's men push the great cross into Thomas' hands. He leans it against his shoulder and steadies himself to take the burden. Still, I won't meet his gaze. He is my brother no longer. All around me, people are jostling to see, to shout derision at Thomas, to rid themselves of the fear of punishment. They look from him to me, and I see them arguing with themselves, wondering how it would go for them if they were ever caught in wrong-doing. Many I think, would choose exile. Many more are silently pledging to remain good and noble all their lives-long. My boys... they'll uphold the law, uphold their tithing, resist temptation and damnation. They will, I know it.

Gilbert and Little Walter spit at Thomas' feet, at the back of his smock, then they turn their backs to him. Thomas trudges slowly eastwards, along the dirt road leading out of Burne, his naked feet crunching on frozen grit.

"Come now," Elizabeth beseeches, her weary eyes blinking back tears. I know they're not for Thomas. I nod, my eyes still fixed on the marsh road and Thomas' receding form.

My boy John hands me my walking-cane, fashioned by Hugh from a twist of seasoned-oak. I accept it gratefully and Hugh lets go of my shoulder. My boy John hurries round to my other side and pushes his head up into my armpit. He's telling me I can lean on him. And I will. I lean more heavily on the walking-stick, though. I do not want to crush my boy. Together we hobble back up the road towards home, Elizabeth following with young Hugo.

They called it leniency when they cut my foot from my body and cast it into the fire. I glance down at the stump of my leg, severed at the ankle, fresh blood pooling on the linen bandaging. I can almost feel my ghost-toes itching.

Rather that, they said, than the gallows.

Rather that, Elizabeth said, than exile.

Cavaliers and Wheatears
Christmas 1685

Memorial stones in the South Chancel aisle of St. Mary's Church are dedicated to the Wilson Family of Eastbourne: To Sir William Wilson, 1st Baronet of Eastbourne and his wife Mary; to their eldest son William, the 2nd Baronet of Eastbourne and his wife Rechard; to their daughter Rechard and their son William, the 3rd Baronet of Eastbourne. The Wilson's resided at Bourne Place (now Compton Place) from 1642-1724 and were staunch royalists throughout the English Civil War. Many of their household papers were scrutinised by the Rev. Walter Budgen in the early twentieth century and presented in his classic historical work 'Old Eastbourne'. Bourne Place was an Elizabethan House, originally built in the classical 'E' style with a long range, and side and central wings. The house has been developed over the years by successive owners and the remaining original portions of Bourne Place lie embedded somewhere within the inner walls of Compton Place.

This is the story of the first Wilson family of Bourne Place and their subtle attempts to subvert the Protectorate and restore the Monarchy, seen through the eyes of their second daughter, Philadelphia Wilson.

other believed that a good game pie was a cure for all ills. We used to laugh at that, after all, the pie was not much of a cure-all for the creatures it contained. It was worse when the pies were made with wheatears. The gamekeepers and shepherds up on the Downs would string up great snares and wait for the migrating birds to fly into them, when they were at their weakest, exhausted and hungry from their long journey home. As a soft-hearted girl, I used to try and protect some of those tiny wild birds, I would find them entangled in the nets and soothe them, unravel the netting from their delicate wings. I could not save them all, for their meat was prized, but those few I found flew free.

The first King Charles once had a game pie presented to him at a feast and when they cut the crust off, a dwarf hopped out, armed with a sword and buckler! As children, we would play the scene out: the king at the table – that was often William, though I myself enjoyed the role; the courtiers – Judith was always the best-dressed; the servants, musicians, jugglers and jesters – the little ones would take turns. John was an excellent juggler and could play the lute very convincingly, Thomas was most often the jester, Edward and Ann would fill in whatever roles needed filling, though Edward was often the funniest dwarf.

We'd sing a little verse too, though by now I have forgotten if we heard it or adapted it ourselves. There were many other versions circulating, so it is a measure of our time that any such songs have survived the years. We began, as many others did, with the tossing of a sixpence to the minstrel (John).

> Sing a song of sixpence,
> a pocket full of rye,
> a sword-wielding dwarf
> did jump out of a pie!

They served the same king a pie filled with live rooks once, and when the crust was taken off, the huge black birds flew out. I imagine they all flew excreting and screeching and flying for the rafters, only to be caught again later for another pie that they did not fly free from. I have never liked that story so well.

A good game pie, mother said, is filled with the creatures of the wild: with pigeons or rooks, larks, or wheatears; with forest buck or tender coney. There are those who call it the Hunter's Pie but that is only partly true, for cooks the country over add tamed-birds to their pies - partridge and goose, turkey, and hen – and it cannot be said that these mild creatures need a-hunting, for they waddle up to a person for a handful of grain. Mrs. Parson has perfected the art of skinning the birds without plucking them. She removes the wings, then cuts the skin by the thighs and draws it over the body and head until the bird is quite naked. She removes the bones and all that cannot be eaten and lays them in the dish to be covered with strips of red meat, salt and pepper, butter, and stock.

Her stock is quite famous: simmered bones and meat scraps, carrots and onions, thyme and parsley and the heady spices of the Orient, Spice Islands and West Indies combined. It is her particular spice blend that places her pies in such esteem and even I do not know the precise recipe, though I often detect cinnamon and ginger and a pinch or two of allspice. Later, she removes the bones, adds port and brandy, and an extra twist of nutmeg. The whole dish is topped with lardy pastry and a glaze of egg wash and baked for a good long while in the oven.

Old Mrs. Parson's stock is simmering in the kitchen now in preparation for the Christmas feast tomorrow. The spice aromas are drifting through all the rooms of the house, creating a season of their own – a season of remembrance - for these smells have ever signalled festivities (and the years when they were forbidden).

~

Now these aromas are destined to signal something else altogether. Father was buried this week alongside mother in their tomb at St. Mary's Church. It was a night procession for him, a mourning in the dark. We followed him to church for the last time, sitting sedately in the coaches as the horses trotted slowly along the road from Bourne Place to the parish church. Forty or so villagers lined the route with flaming torches, and the church when we arrived was sombre with black wreaths and draperies. I never witnessed such a solemn passing before. We left father behind at the night-shrouded church and made our way back to the empty house, now barren of its Baronet.

Father commissioned the engraver to make a black marble tombstone to lie above him and mother in memoriam. Now it is positioned at the East end of the South Chancel aisle, inscribed so:

> Heere lieth interr'd ye body of Sr
> William Wilson Bart who departed
> this life Decr ye 9th 1685 aged 77 yrs.

> Heere lieth also the body of
> Mary ye lady of the said Sr. Willm
> Wilson who was Buried
> Oct. ye 3rd 1661.

Either side of our parents, in the tomb below the church, are vacant spaces lying in wait for father's eldest son and eldest grandson, which is the way with families such as ours. Where I will lie when I am gone, I do not know.

A plaque above their tomb now bears our arms and motto *"Pro Legibus ac Regibus"*: "For Laws and Kings". William and Mary Wilson are proud to announce their allegiance to the crown now their loyalty can no longer be of harm to them. We remaining Wilson's are royalists by default, even when it passes across our minds that the reformers are not all wrong and the monarchs are not all good.

My younger brother William is to become the second Baronet of Eastbourne now father has gone, and the new Lord of Bourne Place. The notion sits strangely with me still, for what is Bourne Place without father? These last two weeks have left an empty feeling in the house, though there are people enough in it. Rechard, Ann and I nursed father through his final days and gave him all the attentions he could desire. His ending was good, as endings go, and it was surely his time: he has been waiting to follow mother these past twenty-four years, it is a wonder to me that he went on so long without her.

Such dreary thoughts plague me today, even as we prepare for the festivities to come. Mother and father did love a celebration. There is something about a funeral that makes me fond of life and I am glad in a way that we are together, as we have not been for a while.

William, with his wife Rechard and his children, young Philadelphia, young William and little Rechard will host the feast of course. Judith has left us already, eager to get back to her children, they'll be spending the season with her second husband's mother. She is still a little ashamed, I think, of marrying so secretly and without father's blessing. I wish she would forget the shadows of the past and spend her time with us. I am decided to stay on awhile at the house and surround myself with family and memories.

Thomas, troubled Thomas, died last year, even before his son was born, though little Thomas is well, we hear, and happy enough with his mother Ann, at Whiligh. Our brother Edward, now Rector of Blatchington, will stay for the feasts, as will John, and Ann, who still resides at Bourne Place though she is nearly at her thirtieth year. We are late to marry, the four of us, and make an unusual gathering. Perhaps we are all still waiting for a love like our parents shared.

The spice aromas are drifting into my chamber, stirring up the spirit of my youth. I feel time contracting, and the years shrinking, and it does not seem like one continuing path from cradle to grave but all things lived at once. I can see mother's face before me so vividly and hear her voice in my ear: another pie is cooking in the oven, and I am barely fourteen. How is it that smells stir up the years so?

~

We were all home and Mrs. Parson was preparing a feast for the weekend. It was a wet and gloomy Easter Week in the year 1658, father was suffering from the gout and groaning in his bed, and we were all a little restless, cooped up in the house like caged birds. Mother was busy with preparations for Easter Sunday and making provisions for the poor of the parish with Mrs. Parson and Judith. I was not yet considered old enough to be of use to mother nor young enough to feel like a child and I rankled at the fog closing in on the windows, darkening the hallways and corridors.

When the dragoons arrived, banging so loud on the door, they startled each of us from our occupations. They insisted on searching the house for evidence of father's royalist plotting and they would have come straight up the stairs to rifle through father's papers if mother hadn't convinced them that they needed rest and refreshment after their long ride from London. She ushered them to the kitchen, as we huddled at the top of stairs, alert to danger, and proffered them the wheatear pie Mrs. Parson had lately baked.

Royalists received short shrift in those days, and should father have been compromised, he would have been taken to the Tower at the very least. Many royalists had swung from the noose at Tower Hill since Charles I had been executed and the men downstairs had been sent by one who had signed his death warrant – Colonel Ingoldsby, cousin to Oliver Cromwell – we knew what was at stake.

While the men were downstairs eating, mother came swiftly upstairs and fetched father's papers from his closet. We burned what needed burning, stoking the fire so it consumed the words that condemned him, stirring the ashes so no trace of conspiracy remained. There was nothing left for Lieutenant Hopkin's dragoons to find by the time they had finished the pie and so it is said that the wheatear pie saved us from Cromwell's army.

Was it the pie I wonder, that saved father, or mother's dogged loyalty? I tend to think the latter, but time tells its own stories. I hear my niece telling the story in her own way and in her version, the pie is the hero.

~

Looking back over the years, I see that we Wilson's were all entangled in the divisive affairs at the heart of the Civil War, but it was my parents who embodied the struggle. Civil war broke out in 1642, the year my parents married and ended the year my mother died. The first King Charles – whom my parents defended – was beheaded in 1649, the year my baby brother Francis was born and died. The dragoons came to our house for wheatear pie and a bellyful of failure in 1658, the year that Oliver Cromwell died. My mother died in 1661, the year that Charles II was crowned, and he has died this very year – 1685 – the same one that my father has left us in. See how the years define us so?

I have heard all manner of rumour concerning William and Mary Wilson. For people often whisper in the dark these days in search of people to fear or people to blame. It is said that my father was a member of the Sealed Knot. I cannot confirm or repudiate such a claim, though it could be said that he had allegiances with their cause and that he was not unknown to their number. Perhaps it was a coincidence that three imprisoned members of that secret society – one of them now a proven collaborator with Cromwell's spymaster Thurloe – were released from the Tower a few weeks before the dragoons came knocking at our house. I could not say with complete certainty whether father was working towards an uprising against Cromwell while assisting in a landing of Charles Stuart the younger in Sussex with an armed force from Flanders. But it is possible.

I have heard it told that kings have been, at one time or other, sequestered in some nook or priest hole at Bourne Place, yet to my knowledge, neither the first nor the second Charles Stuart ever set foot in this house, though they would have been welcomed as they fled Cromwell's army or should they ever have needed to return this way.

It is not just father who the whisperers whisper about. Mother had her own secrets, as did her stepfather Dr. Burton, who sold this house to our parents. He was once a chaplain to Charles the First and was furious at his regicide. He had the tombstone carver etch his own epitaph to let it be known that he was 'always a hater and smiter of Presbyterians', Presbyterianism being very strong in Scotland and it having been the Scots who handed Charles I over to the English Parliament. Yet it was only when the Presbyterians were expelled from the House of Commons by the Puritan Independents, that the King's trial began in earnest. There have been many complications of faith and belief over these past few years. Perhaps it has been inevitable, since old King Henry VIII caused the schism from Rome over his marriage to Anne Boleyn. All has been unsettled since that time.

The second King Charles's death has shaken the easeful feeling that fell over the land at the ending of the civil war. Now his brother James Stuart has claimed the throne – and he has already put to death his own nephew, James of Monmouth, to ensure his ascension. The tensions are rising, I hear whispers of conspiracy and split allegiances and I sense that the struggle continues, for this new King is Catholic in his tendencies, which makes us all fear another war. The Catholic's are small in number in England these days and their religion is unwelcome. There is much talk too, of the Divine Right of Kings, of the assumption of power based on birth and the spread of power through parliament. I do not know how we would face another war, but I do know that we will not know peace in our lives whilst these men of power struggle amongst themselves.

It is well, that father will not have to live through more monarchical turmoil. His time, like mother's, was spent serving the Charles Stuarts, in defiance of the Protectorate and those few men who would destroy a kingdom to reform it in their own interests. I feel that my time will be served in the defiance of Catholicism and Protestantism, walking the moderate Anglican *via media* that my father set us on, for it is at the extremes of faith where conflict rages. It seems that there is something to defy in every lifetime.

~

Even the little wheatears I longed to defend have much to defy, as they battle for survival each year on their perilous journey north. Whenever I find myself in Bourne during the spring season, I stand awhile on the Downs and watch the seaward skies for the sight of their return. Black-headed gulls, herring gulls, oyster catchers and rooks frequent these shores and I see more of them by the sea than any other bird. Some of those I see are destined for Mrs. Parson's pot and yet I do not mourn them so much as I do the wheatears. It is not that the black-cheeked, white-arsed chats are the heroes of the tale, though the pie no doubt helped father's cause, it is that the tiny birds defy all expectation to do what must be done. There is a tenacity in their natural behaviour that I admire.

My mother was that way, tenacious and defiant, strong in heart and mind. She was our friend and confidante, our conscience, and our reasoning, she was our life and we hers. Father became a baronet the year Charles II was crowned, after mother had advised him to send a gift of Wilson-estate wheatears for the king's delectation, in celebration of his return to the monarchy. Mother was a Baroness for just three months before she died, which was a cruel trick for life to play on her.

I am here at Bourne Place so little these days, I prefer the London life, and truly this is now a house for future baronets, not old maids. Still, while I have a tongue in my head, we will not eat wheatears within these walls.

Christmas will be a strange affair this year, so close to father's death, but this is the season for merry-making, no matter what the remaining puritans believe, and we must make an effort to put on a little cheer and entertainment. The hall and parlour have been delightfully decorated by Rechard and the children, who have been practicing their songs for a fireside rendition. Old Mrs. Parson's pie will be centre stage on the table and there are to be mince pies, roast partridge and plover, braised beef, and plum pottage. There'll be plenty to share with William's tenants when they arrive, and we will make something of the season. A good game pie cannot cure all ills, but it can certainly raise the spirits.

I have in mind the verses we sang with the little ones in the years following father's narrow escape from the Tower, they were a salve in the times when we wished for our mother to appear, though she could not. They remind me of games in the parlour, of kings and their foibles, of loyalty and laughter. If I close my eyes a little, I can dream of the first Christmas that presaged the end of the Protectorate.

We gathered the chairs around the fire and dressed ourselves in old costumes: Judith played mother – bustling; William played father – groaning in a makeshift bed; and the rest of us set bowls upon our heads and held pokers against our shoulders as we sang our parents their very own verse.

> Sing a song of sixpence,
> a pocket full of rye,
> six dragoons with muskets
> lingered round a pie
>
> When the pie was opened,

The children sat whisp'ring,
Wasn't that the neatest trick
To play upon Hopkins?

Father was in his chamber
Fending off the gout,
Mother was in the kitchen
Handing game pie out

Those letters in the fire
Curled crisply into dust,
As soldiers sat downstairs and ate
The crumbly pastry crust.

When the pie was over,
And all were done supping,
They wandered up the stairs too late
To find a single thing –

Off they left for London,
Dragoons without a clue
And Bourne Place saw the last of them
With a horse's backside view.

When the pie was digested,
We swore we heard them fart,
As trotting up the Old Town Road
They swiftly did depart.

Mary and William Wilson
Were then heard loud to sing
"Cromwell's men can't hold us back
from fighting for our king!"

Philadelphia Wilson, Bourne Place 1685

WHEEL OF FORTUNE

The Thomas Wilson Affair:
A Play in One Act

The Lamb Inn, on the High Street in Old Town, is a fourteenth century building that became a fifteenth century Coaching Inn. The Lamb is renowned for its blackened timber beams and white walls, its ancient cellar with vaulted undercroft, and a deep well whose depths disappear beneath the Inn's foundations. A timber-framed house known as The Greys once stood on Greys Road, behind the still-standing medieval house of Pilgrims on Borough Lane and was home to the Scarlett's of Eastbourne. The Inn, The Greys, Pilgrims, the Old Parsonage, the Parsonage Barn and St. Mary's Church next to the Inn, formed a core of historical buildings that were well known to the Wilson's of Bourne Place. Thomas Wilson, the fourth and most disruptive son of William Wilson, the 1st Baronet of Eastbourne, needed the particular aid of the Scarlett family during a strange incident which was documented in the annals of the Wilson estate. The first William Wilson, in his will and testament, left a provocative caveat to Thomas's inheritance – that it was to be withheld until such time as Thomas could prove himself to be 'a civil and orderly person, fit to employ and manage money'.

This play script is set in the bar room of the Lamb Inn in the early eighteenth century and centres on a group of customers and the Landlord and his wife as they discuss the curious Thomas Wilson affair.

he year is 1724, the month is October. Two men are sitting around a table in the ancient Lamb Inn in Eastbourne. The Innkeeper is tending the bar and his wife is working in the kitchen. The Inn is lit by candlelight and oil lamps. Pipe smoke gathers in a fug near the low-beamed ceiling, a fire burns brightly in the hearth. A brown-eared spaniel lies on a bed near the fire, his drying fur adding to the room's aroma. Outside, the rain is pouring down in the early dark of this autumn evening. Through misted, latticed windows, the lamplit street outside can be glimpsed.

Characters:

Tom Bragge:	Parish Clerk
George Tucket:	Grocer
Nicholas Crump:	Innkeeper
Charlotte Crump:	Innkeeper's wife
Abel Wotton:	Ex-servant at Bourne Place

The Play:

Tom Bragge:	…He's selling the mansion to Spencer Compton.
Nicholas Crump:	Who is?
Tom Bragge:	Sir Thomas Wilson, the fourth Baronet.
George Tucket:	Why's he doing that then?
Tom Bragge:	For the money of course and he don't need it does he? He's got that old pile in Uckfield to inherit from his father-in-law and he never expected to take the Baronetcy at all did he?
George Tucket:	Who'd he take it off of?
Tom Bragge:	Sir William Wilson, third Baronet – his great nephew.
Nicholas Crump:	Aye, I heard of young Sir William's death. Nineteen he was, that's no age, is it?
George Tucket:	Which William's that then?
Tom Bragge:	You know… the grandson of Sir William Wilson, the second one.
George Tucket:	The second grandson?
Tom Bragge:	No. the… listen. There was old Sir William – the one who was given the title by Charles the second.
Nicholas Crump:	Aye. He's buried next door.
George Tucket:	True. With his wife Mary. I've seen the inscriptions in the end chapel.
Tom Bragge:	Anyway, his son William…
Nicholas Crump:	The second Baronet
Tom Bragge:	That's what I'm saying.
George Tucket:	Right.
Tom Bragge:	Well his son William. .
George Tucket:	Why they all called William?
Nicholas Crump:	Search me.
Tom Bragge:	…his son William died young, even while William number two was Baronet, and his own grandson William…

George Tucket:	Bloody hell. They could have learned a different name. Like James. What's wrong with James?
Nicholas Crump:	Trying to turn them Jacobite?
George Tucket:	What? No! I'm just saying, that's a lot of Williams.
Tom Bragge:	Aye, but it is what it is. So, this William, who was the grandson of the second William.
Nicholas Crump:	Aye, I'm with you.
Tom Bragge:	He inherited the title and estates when his grandfather died.
George Tucket:	S'alright for some.
Tom Bragge:	Not really... listen.
Nicholas Crump:	When was that then?
Tom Bragge:	Six years ago.
George Tucket:	I did hear of that now you mention it. Just a lad, wasn't he?
Tom Bragge:	Aye, and away at military school. That's why the family let Bourne Place to Spencer Compton.
George Tucket:	The one who's buying it now.
Tom Bragge:	Aye, but you're ahead of yourself. Pipe down a second. The story's confusing enough. You listening?
George Tucket:	[nods]
Tom Bragge:	So, the lad's just died.
George Tucket:	You what? Can't be that old, can he?
Tom Bragge:	Nineteen he was.
George Tucket:	That's no age.
Nicholas Crump:	No, no age at all.
Tom Bragge:	Gor you lot do go on. So, the point is that now it's being sold.
George Tucket:	Bourne Place?
Tom Bragge:	Aye. To Spencer Compton.
Nicholas Crump:	Well, that's that then.
Tom Bragge:	That's what?
Nicholas Crump:	Well, that's the end of summat, in't it? No more Baronets in Eastbourne.
George Tucket:	What's that to us, hey? It don't put bread on our tables to 'ave a honourable sir in our midst, does it?
Tom Bragge:	What you on about? They're the landowners, half the town are their tenants! Besides, Spencer Compton's just as much an honourable as them Wilson's. He's a Whig MP, he is and some-kind of paymaster for the Army. Treasurer for Prince George too – the man's surrounded by money.
Nicholas Crump:	Well, it does good to my coffers to have them honourables about. Good spenders they were, the Wilson's, when they were around. Lord Compton's not much of a drinker but his staff keep us busy.
George Tucket:	Who's selling the house?
Tom Bragge:	You what?

George Tucket:	Well, if the owner just died..
Nicholas Crump:	Poor lad.
George Tucket:	Aye but who's selling it?
Tom Bragge:	The new Sir Thomas Wilson.
George Tucket:	Never met him, who's that then?
Tom Bragge:	He's one of the first Baronet's grandsons.
Nicholas Crump:	Never meant to get the title in the first place was he, this Sir Thomas? Well down the line he was – and his father.
Tom Bragge:	Aye, should have gone to one of the older boy's or their sons. Died though, didn't they.
Nicholas Crump:	Aye, bad luck that.
George Tucket:	Not so great being a sir after all.
Nicholas Crump:	Nah.
George Tucket:	Who was his father then?
Tom Bragge:	Who?
George Tucket:	Sir Thomas Wilson.
Tom Bragge:	Same like him, Thomas Wilson

[The landlord's wife walks in from the back room, a platter of cooked meats and fresh bread in her hands. She puts it down on the table.]

Charlotte Crump:	I met him a couple a times, the first Thomas Wilson. Handsome boy he was, idle as a newt though, you could tell.
Tom Bragge:	Course he was kidnapped by pirates weren't he?
Charlotte Crump:	Ha ah ha! Pulling my leg are you?
Tom Bragge:	No I swear, he was kidnapped, he was, from London and taken off to sea.
Charlotte Crump:	Off to where?
George Crump:	Barbados, I heard.
Tom Bragge:	No you old fool, it was Jamaica.
Nicholas Crump:	Aye, I heard that. Got himself caught up with the wrong sort he did and spent his days hanging round the murkier streets of Southwark.
Charlotte Crump:	They's all murky up there, ent they?
Tom Bragge:	Aye, full of murderers and thieves. They got that Marshalsea prison there, an all them others. Stuffed wi' prisons and stuffed wi' cutthroats and pickpockets. Wouldn't catch me there if yer paid me.
George Tucket:	'S'like he wanted to get into mischief. What's he want to go hanging round there for when he's got a great big house down here?
Nicholas Crump:	You got me.
Tom Bragge:	Cromwell's head was stuck on a pole near there.
Charlotte Crump:	You what?
Tom Bragge:	They dug him up, didn't they, when old prince Charlie got back on the throne. That mad he was, you know 'cause he killed his father an all, that

	they took his head off him and stuck it on a pole at Westminster.
George Tucket:	Is that near Southwark then?
Tom Bragge:	Other side of the Thames.
George Tucket:	Gor, that must've been a right sight.
Nicholas Crump:	Aye.

[The Inn door blows open, bringing the rain and wind with it and a tumult of copper leaves. An aged man walks in, shivers, takes off his dripping coat and hangs it by the fire, ruffling the spaniel's ears as it looks up to greet him.]

Nicholas Crump:	That's it Abel, come on in and take a load off.
Abel Wotton:	Evening all, foul night out there.
Charlotte Crump:	Good evening, Abel.
Abel Wotton:	Charlotte. {Tips his hat}
Nicholas Crump:	Best ale?
Abel Wotton:	Aye, if you please.
George Tucket:	Evening Abel, how's Mary?
Abel Wotton:	Aye, she be well thanks George.

[Abel settles down in a vacant chair.]

Tom Bragge:	Here Abel, you'd know about them rumours... of Thomas Wilson senior's kidnapping...
Abel Wotton:	Aye Tom, that I do, but 'tis more than rumours. I were there at the house when the boy Thomas were a lad, lazy little imp he were, always up to summat too. Restless you might call 'im and no better than he should be.
George Tucket:	You knew the Wilson boy? Fancy that! There's us saying we never saw him.
Nicholas Crump:	Wait no, I never said that. Course I seen him. My father had the Inn then and I saw inside many an evening. Liked his drink he did, and fast talk, and smart-mouthed he were, but rough with it.
Charlotte Crump:	Handsome though.
Nicholas Crump:	You said that already. Have a thing for him did you?
Charlotte Crump:	What? No, just that's what you notice in a person i'nt it?
Nicholas Crump:	Carry on Abel, we'll hear your tale instead of our Charlotte's lustings.
Charlotte Crump:	I am not..
Nicholas Crump:	Speak on Abel.
Abel Wotton:	I worked down at the house for sixty years, I did. Only stopped last year. My back's gone now, you see. Can't bend down for anyone.

{Abel stretches his shoulders and presses his hands to his back, his joints creak.}

Abel Wotton:	Still, it were a good life there.
George Tucket:	Cor, sixty years – did you really?
Abel Wotton:	Aye. Man and boy. Even stayed on after the Wilson's leased the house to Spencer Compton. Course, he didn't want all their old papers and belongings and such, so who do you think had to go through them all and send them off for keeping? That's right, you're looking at him.
Tom Bragge:	What kind of papers?
Abel Wotton:	You know, the usual, letters and deeds and such like. Only, there were a bunch of letters in one of the cabinets that all related to the Jamaican affair. Even one from young Thomas to his father William, letting him know he were gone.
George Tucket:	So, what did the letter say?
Abel Wotton:	Oh, now let me think...

{Abel takes a long draught.}

Abel Wotton:	He said he were a servant for four years and that the labour would like as not be the end of him. Asked his father for money to set him free like.
Tom Bragge:	Did he send it?
Abel Wotton:	Aye, eventually, though he were tempted not to. Thought that maybe it would be the making of young Thomas, the boy hadn't worked a decent day in his life. But then he thought on it and how it can't be that we live in a nation where people can get kidnapped off the streets for profit and that angered him sure enough.
Tom Bragge:	What did he do?
Nicholas Crump:	Did he get the boy back?
George Tucket:	Did he go and fetch him himself? That'd be a long way to go wouldn't it?
Charlotte Crump:	You wouldn't catch me sailing out there.
Abel Wotton:	Well lucky for old Sir William and his son Thomas, there were a way to fetch help to him without that. See that house out there – Pilgrims?

[Abel points out of the nearest window. They all peer through the misted glass at the narrow Borough Lane across from the High Street, with a white and black-timbered house on the corner.]

Abel Wotton:	Well behind Pilgrims, is a house called The Greys, that were the home of the Scarlett's. It so happened that the first Scarlett boy, Francis, was a Captain in the Navy and he had a home in Jamaica.

[Abel looks at each of them in turn, checking he's got his audience with him. He drains his drink and studies the empty tankard.]

Nicholas Crump:	Here, let me top that up for you.
Abel Wotton:	Thank ee kindly. Where was I? Oh, aye, the Scarlett's. Been disinherited Francis had, his father had left all his wealth to his younger son who he got with his second wife. So, you can imagine how that would have gone down with young Francis, but he was one of them getting-on-with-it types, and he made no quarrel with his brother. Made himself a pile of money out on the island after we took it from the Spaniards, had himself plantations growing sugar, coffee, and tobacco. Brought some home with him now and then he did and then we could all get a taste of them West Indies.
Tom Bragge:	So, Captain Francis went and fetched Thomas?
Abel Wotton:	It weren't that easy to be sure. You see, they might not have taken 'im fair and square from London but by the time they got him out to Jamaica, they got a contract signed up – all legal like.
Nicholas Crump:	Well, they could have just bought him out of it.
George Tucket:	Aye, that's how things are done.
Abel Wotton:	And he tried, Francis did. I heard it from his lips. He found the plantation they were keeping him at, but it was seven months since Thomas' letter had been sent and he didn't know what to expect. Well, when Francis got there, there was no master in sight. Died he had, a few months before, and Thomas was living up at the old master's house with his comely widow.
Tom Bragge:	Oh aye?
George Tucket:	Little beggar.
Abel Wotton:	Aye, and she were right smitten with him and didn't like to let him go. Do you know, she'd given him all sorts of positions...

[George snorts.]

Abel Wotton:	...he were made an overseer, bailiff and steward and he were like a lord over them other slaves. And Francis says to him that his father Sir William sends his regards, and she goes spitting feathers, this widow, cause she didn't know she'd been housing gentry and she'd been wanting to keep him, though he'd told her he were married and couldn't stay around. And she realised – too late – that she was letting a real prize slip from her grip.
Nicholas Crump:	Ha! What a merry widow! Didn't miss her

	husband then...
George Tucket:	Aye, a merry widow till she lost her new paramour.
Tom Bragge:	Well Thomas was free then and made it home?
Abel Wotton:	Not quite. You see, Jamaica's not as easy-going a place as they make it out to be. Sure, the sun's hot and the fields are fertile, and the crops grow like weeds, but it's infested with bad folk, no-good sorts what'd kill yer soon as look at yer.
George Tucket:	Why's that then?

[Abel stretches his legs out, gives a protracted sigh.]

Abel Wotton:	All them nations out fighting for the same territories, all that sea trade going back and forth from the Americas back here. Everyone's fighting everyone for what each other's got. Sailors turned privateers and pirates, soldiers turned landowners and farmers, slaves being bought and sold all over and everyone trying to make a profit from everyone else.
Tom Bragge:	Lawless it is.
George Tucket:	Aye, lawless, you said it in one. They ain't civilised out there.
Nicholas Crump:	Specially not now they send all them prisoners over there. 'Tis nothing but a penal colony.
Charlotte Crump:	Where?
Nicholas Crump:	You know.. tobacco country. Virginia.
Charlotte Crump:	Oh. So is that where Thomas went? To Virginia?
Nicholas Crump:	Why would he go there?
Abel Wotton:	He didn't go there. He stayed on Jamaica. Sir William...
George Tucket:	The first one?
Abel Wotton:	Aye... Sir William hadn't actually sent the money over, couldn't risk it you see what with all them pirates running the harbour, so he ordered Captain Francis to take the money from the old Governor of Jamaica and he'd pay him back like.
Tom Bragge:	That's a lot to ask a man.
Abel Wotton:	Well, them men of Jamaica had plenty of it, you see? Only problem was, once the old Governor bought Thomas from the widow ..
George Tucket:	Aye, go on.
Abel Wotton:	...well he kept him as a servant.
Nicholas Crump:	Ha ah! So, it didn't go so easy for Thomas! Bet he wished he stayed with the widow!
George Tucket:	Aye, if you've got to be a servant, might as well enjoy it.
Abel Wotton:	That's not how it went.
Tom Bragge:	Who was this Governor then?

Abel Wotton:	Sir Thomas Modyford.
Tom Bragge:	Oh, that makes a difference.
George Tucket:	Heard of him have you?
Tom Bragge:	Who hasn't? Remember when he was put in the Tower of London with that pirate...what's his name?
Nicholas Crump:	Henry Morgan. [Spits on the fire.]
Tom Bragge:	Aye, the Spanish were out for their blood after he sacked Panama, just after they signed that peace treaty an' all.
George Tucket:	That were a lifetime ago.
Abel Wotton:	True. But Thomas Modyford made it back to Jamaica with the King's pardon in his ear.
Tom Bragge:	And then he goes and buys our Thomas from the widow.
Abel Wotton:	Aye.
George Tucket:	I need a drink.
Nicholas Crump:	Coming right up.
Tom Bragge:	Throw another log on the fire, would you?

[George banks the fire and they all settle down again, each of them taking a long drink in the brief silence]

Charlotte Crump:	How did he get home then, after that?
Abel Wotton:	Well, it took a while. Modyford put him to work overseeing the other slaves on his plantation and young Thomas suffered again. Cause he thought of himself as a free man by then. And when a man's suffering, he does what he can to make things better, and him being an overseer – and from a family of Baronets - he thinks of himself as way above them like, but they don't see it like that and he gets a few roughin's-up by them.
George Tucket:	How'd you know that?
Abel Wotton:	Sir Thomas Modyford. He sent a letter to old Sir William.
Tom Bragge:	He did?
George Tucket:	What did it say?
Abel Wotton:	I'm telling you already. It said that young Thomas was complaining of not having enough freedom nor enough money and he needed money on account of how the other men ripped his shirt off his back. And that was another debt coming Sir William's way.
George Tucket:	Was that it?
Abel Wotton:	Well, no. You see, Sir William had secretly asked Sir Thomas Modyford to keep young Thomas on the island and set him to work with a merchant, to earn his keep like. But you'll remember that Thomas didn't like to work.

[George and Tom nod.]

Abel Wotton:	That's why young Thomas kept getting himself in mischief, you see. Too lazy for his own good.
George Tucket:	Nowt ever comes good of a lazy man.
Tom Bragge:	I reckon he changed his ways eventually.
George Tucket:	Why'd you say that?
Tom Bragge:	Well, he married well, didn't he?
George Tucket:	Did he?
Tom Bragge:	Aye.
Charlotte Crump:	But how'd he get off the island?
Abel Wotton:	Modyford wrote to Captain Scarlett. Tells him the boy's nothing but trouble and he wants to pay for him to be sent home!
George Tucket:	Blimey. He must've been a right one.
Tom Bragge:	Still, he was kidnapped an' all. It's not like he chose to go and work out there.
Nicholas Crump:	Aye, kidnapping's a rum business.

[George chortles.]

George Tucket:	Jamaican rum?
Nicholas Crump:	It's good that.
George Tucket:	Sends your head blind.
Tom Bragge:	You'd know.
George Tucket:	So that was that then? Kidnapped and returned. Sounds like he could've been better though, you know what I mean? Like he needed a lesson to sort him out. P'rhaps a kidnapping was the making of him.
Tom Bragge:	Aye, that's what I were saying. He married well, a daughter of George Courthope of Whiligh, and they had their children.
Nicholas Crump:	One of whom was our Thomas.
Tom Bragge:	Aye. But his luck ran out you see, cause old Thomas never even met his lad before he died.
George Tucket:	Now that's unlucky. What a family!
Tom Bragge:	Aye. Now our Sir Thomas Wilson's inherited his grandfather's title and estate and he's selling off the estate to Spencer Compton.
Nicholas Crump:	Who's already been living there for six years.
Tom Bragge:	Aye.
George Tucket:	Well, that is a good story, though no one comes out of it very well.
Tom Bragge:	'Tis a shame. Though they had their wealth to rely on.
George Tucket:	Aye, they'd that, though I reckon they'd have traded it for better fortune.
Tom Bragge:	You do?

George Tucket:	Sure, except I don't think wealthy folk could handle life without all their money.
Tom Bragge:	You could be right.
Abel Wotton:	He's changing the name of it, you know?
Tom Bragge:	Who?
Abel Wotton:	Spencer Compton. He's calling the house 'Compton Place'.
George Tucket:	Ooh. Fancy. Mayhap I should call my home 'Tucket Place'. Aye, I'll do that. From now on you can call me George Tucket of Tucket Place.
Nicholas Crump:	Hah! Be after a fortune next, you will.
George Tucket:	No not me. Happy with what I got, I am.
Abel Wotton:	Best way that is.
Tom Bragge:	I'm a light candle on Sunday.
George Tucket:	For the Wilson's?
Tom Bragge:	Aye, I'll set it down in front of that memorial of theirs and send 'em some prayers. Sounds like they need 'em, don't it?
Abel Wotton:	You're a good man, Tom, that you are.
George Tucket:	Shall we have another round?
Tom Bragge:	Aye, let's have another.
George Tucket:	And we'll have a drink for them that's departed and them that remains and may we all live long enough to enjoy good fortune.
Tom Bragge:	Aye, and a drink for good friends, good ale, and good cheer.

[The dog barks. Outside, the wind howls, the table-candle waivers, and smokes. The fire crackles, rain spatters hard on the windows and the men sit back in their seats, glad of the company and the warmth, ready to discuss less weighty matters - the harvest, price of market goods, the weather. We leave them behind in the convivial warmth of the Lamb Inn by the Church of St. Mary's in the Old Town by the Bourne stream.]

A Fracas at Foxholes
December 1824

astbourne was prepared for a Napoleonic invasion that never came. The Martello towers and Redoubt Fortress were garrisoned in 1805, and temporary camps were constructed on the downs. Napoleon's army was defeated in 1815 but the watch towers and fortress remained. Far from being the end of the country's troubles, the close of war brought joblessness and higher taxes, which forced some former militia to seek their fortunes in the smuggling trade. Other ex-militia joined the Coastal Blockade Service to prevent smuggling. The post-war smuggling boom was so prolific that by 1822, Coastguard Watch Houses were built at Cuckmere Haven, Crowlink Gap, and Holywell to deter smugglers. In 1828, a temporary wooden lighthouse was built on Beachy Head to protect shipping off the rocky shore, but these coastal defences and protections weren't strong enough to stop the trade in un-taxed goods. By 1832, coastguard cottages had been built next to the Watchhouses to allow more men to be stationed at the smuggling zones, and the granite Belle Tout lighthouse was finished. In less than thirty years, the coastline of Eastbourne had become heavily fortified against the threat of war and smuggling from across the channel, and against the threat of wreckage on the rocky shore for ships carrying taxable goods.

This story is based on a genuine court case that was reported in the Morning Post on Tuesday 28th December 1824 and follows the trial of Thomas Mills and his accuser William Williamson through to its conclusion

illiam Williamson hobbled into the courtroom on crutches, assisted by some of his former shipmates. Mr. Justice Burrough allowed him a chair and he settled awkwardly, scanning the room for familiar faces. All eyes in the room returned his gaze, drawn to the livid red scars that crossed his brow and puckered his cheek. William's lawyer, Mr. Knox, faced the jury and informed them that William Williamson had been a seaman of his Majesty's ship *Ramillies*, which lay at anchor in the Downs "..the harbour on the North Sea, not the chalk hills of Sussex!" he explained, which caused a titter of amusement. Mr. Williamson, he told the court, had been stationed onshore at Crowlink, near Cuckmere Haven, acting in the assistance of Lieutenant Woodham of the Royal Naval Coast Blockade Service, on the night in question. He had, in the course of his duties, been active in the prevention of smuggling on the Sussex coast.

Thomas Mills of Seaford was being charged under indictment, Mr. Knox informed the Court, at these Lewes Winter Assizes with no less than nine counts of felony: having allegedly maimed, wounded, and hurt said William Williamson, in the course of assembling with a number of other armed persons, for the purpose of aiding in the landing of un-customed goods. He stood in the stand with his head down, after a fleeting glimpse at William's ruined face.

Mr. Andrews, lawyer for the defence, waited for his turn to question the witness, and the jury watched impassively. William listened to Mr. Knox explaining the circumstances of the events that took place on the 31st of July of the previous year.

~

He recalled the day only too well; an unseasonably cold summer evening in 1823. There had been a long twilight lasting well past nine. He had been stationed on the east side of the Cuckmere River, standing as motionless as he could in the cold, deep shadows of the cliff. Against the dark sky, a chill, sepia-toned moon had shone clear and silvery across the waves, as it traced a westward arc through the stars.

The scene had mesmerised him; brought him to another time some nine years before, and another full moon on the other side of the ocean, some thousand leagues from home. It had been the same year Napoleon was exiled to Elba, and France temporarily restored its monarchy - 1814 - two years since the outbreak of the United States war against the British, its dependent colonies in North America, and the Native Americans. *Ramillies* had been at anchor off Connecticut; William with his pistol in hand, held a flaming torch ready to hurl at the ink-black ships in the bay. There had been gunfire and canon fire, swarms of American soldiers and British sailors: all appearing the same under the light of the sepia-moon.

They had been repelled, failed to sack Stonington, and destroy the shipping fleet, but ten days later, the British had burnt the White House in Washington to the ground. He really wasn't sure who'd won that war, but the war against Napoleon that raged for another year had been decisive enough.

That night at the Cuckmere, as a wave of clouds billowed across the sky, he barely noticed the moon sink beyond its zenith from his shadowed-hide on the beach; small wonder he hadn't noticed the boat row by.

A bang from the direction of the river mouth startled him back to his senses. The echoing crack and flash of pistol blasts reverberated round the cliff walls. He did not hesitate. He raced across the beach, skid-sliding on pebbles to the river's edge and up along the eastern bank, past moonlit reed beds, rivulets, and saltmarsh and up beside the wide channel of the Cuckmere in the shadow of the Downs, to catch up with the boatmen who had glided past his watch.

"I ran to a spot called Foxholes, where I saw a cart and several men standing about thirty feet from the boat," William explained to Mr. Knox, to judge and jury. "I observed men round the boat employed in throwing tubs ashore. I was standing about twelve yards from the boat for a minute or two to look at them and saw that each man carried a bludgeon." He shuffled in his seat, flexed his leg. "I seized a man coming out of the boat, but he immediately dealt a heavy blow to my belly with an oar."

The oar had winded him, and the man had slipped from his grasp and run off towards the cart. He had lunged then for another man, who knocked him down with a punch to the jaw and they scuffled. The man in his grasp, terrified and wild, had lashed out at him and he, afraid for his life, pulled his pistol free and fired. The shot, though wide, had startled the man who fell to his knees with his fists bunched in prayer, crying "Lord have mercy upon me!" It was then that William noticed Thomas Mills amongst the gang – Deaf Tom as he knew him – a local man he often met on the beach and who was well known to him by sight.

He had stood there by the swift-flowing river in the half-light of the early morning, unknown faces surrounding him, half-hidden in shadows. He had enough shot for half the smugglers, if need be, but the other half...

"Well, well, well, if we haven't gone and got ourselves a little guardsman all alone in the world," someone had said, stepping forward and shining a half-damped lantern in his face, blinding him for a moment.

"And us with all these tubs to clear," someone else said.

"Ere, I know him Joh-!" Thomas Mills called out.

"-Shut your hole man! No names – I told you – no witnesses neither. You ain't so deaf you don't know that."

"Here boys, I think we should get out of here," another voice loud-whispered.

"So, says you, but I see a whole different outcome-." The voice, grating and low, rasped before him. The lantern appeared so near to his face, its flame scorched his beard. He could feel the other men surrounding him, closing in. "-one where we get to carry on our business, quiet like. If you're all of my mind, I'll be damned if we leave a single tub for them." Raising his bludgeon high, the man cracked it down on William's arm, a blow that knocked the pistol from his hand. The shadowy figures advanced as one, bludgeons, fists and feet aimed at every part of his person.

"What'll we do with this pesky bluecoat?" someone shouted.

"Cut his damned throat," someone else answered.

A silver blade shone sharply in the moonlight, aimed at his head.

The courtroom was a sea of eager faces waiting for the rest of the story. William eased his leg out, stretching it in front of him until it clicked. He leaned on his crutch, feeling suddenly exhausted. It did not take much these days to tire him out. There was something about the eagerness with which the room absorbed his tale that unsettled him; they wanted all the details. He absently rubbed the scar on his brow, tracing the puckers and folds where the skin had healed unevenly over the wounds.

Surely the men in the Court could work out for themselves what had happened, as they side-glanced at his tapered leg and scarred face. Thomas Mills, across the room, sat rosy-cheeked and hale. But that night, he had been a terrified face among the crowd.

"What happened next, Mr. Williamson?" Mr. Knox urged.

"Yes, speak up man," the Judge added irritably.

~

The knife had descended.

William knocked the blade away, but a bludgeon caught him full on the cheek. His head whipped back. Fists and sticks pummelled him but there was no sound other than ringing, loud and insistent. A fist to his jaw flipped him backwards and for a breath or two everything was silent and still, but the punches were relentless.

His foot connected with someone's shin. He rolled over to avoid a bludgeon strike and barrelled two men from their feet, reached out blindly, tearing fabric, scratching skin, ducking from blows. If he got round behind them..., could he run?

A thrust to his chest cracked a rib, maybe more, a blade in his shoulder hit bone. A foot connected with his thigh. Something snapped. Another blow to his head sent him sprawling and a shadowy fist brought the silver blade down again and again.

"Williams and Fleming-" He indicated two of his shipmates who had helped him into the courtroom. "-appeared from across the river and the smugglers, on seeing them, ran."

"And you informed these men that you knew one Thomas Mills among the smugglers?" Mr. Knox asked.

"Yes Sir, I told them straight away. Deaf Tom it was and there he is." He raised his finger towards Thomas Mills, slouching in the dock.

Mr. Knox addressed the jury, advising them to observe William Williamson's condition and to note his absolute assurance that the man standing accused before them all was indeed a smuggler of the lowest sort.

Mr. Andrews, for the Defence, took to the room and sauntered over to William. "Can you say for certain who struck you? Did the prisoner strike you?"

William thought back to the morning, what he had seen, what he hadn't seen. He couldn't swear that the prisoner had struck him. He had been surrounded by several men, but he had not specifically seen the prisoner dealing any blows.

"The men stabbed me, dragged me, kicked me and trampled upon me, but I do not know the names of those who struck me, though there were ten or twelve of them."

"Tell us, when did you next see the prisoner?"

"Three days later, at my bedside, accompanying Lieutenant Woodham for questioning. I knew him instantly to be the same person whom I saw on the night of the affray, and whom I described by the name of Deaf Tom."

"And on the night in question, did you or did you not lose consciousness from your injuries?"

"I, uh, yes..."

"I see, and yet three days later you could recall all the details of the night with absolute clarity?"

"Why yes, I know what I saw."

"Thank you, Mr. Williams, that will be all."

William was assisted from his chair and helped to a seat at the front of the court as Thomas Williams, fellow Blockade man, took the stand. They had served together on the *Ramillies*, even as she guarded the harbour at Portsmouth after the Napoleonic war, and together they had joined the Coastal Blockade stationed at Crowlink.

~

Thomas Williams, examined by the prosecution, had been stationed on the west side of the Cuckmere River on the night in question. "Between one and two o'clock I saw a boat come in. I hailed her and fired my pistol. Fleming came to my assistance and the boat rowed upriver. It pulled in at Foxhole Head. I heard a noise of people talking together and saw Williamson running along the opposite side of the river. I saw a pistol fired and Williamson skirmishing with more than a dozen men. I had to swim across the river to reach him and by the time we-" he indicated towards Richard Fleming, seated beside William Williamson. "-got there the smugglers were gone. Williamson was lying there in the mud, his head all cut open and his face covered with blood."

"What did you do next?"

"I tied my handkerchief round his head, which roused him some, and he told me Deaf Tom was there. I do not myself know Deaf Tom."

"Was there any evidence of un-customed goods on the boat?"

"I found two tubs within and seventeen more outside of her."

"Can you speak to what these tubs contained?"

"They contained gin."

"And what happened to these tubs?"

"I brought them to the Cuckmere Watchhouse with the boat and gave them over to Lieutenant Sankey."

All he had to add when cross-examined by Mr. Andrews was that he had been fifty fathoms from Williamson when he saw him attacked by the smugglers, but it had been quite possible to see him across the river. The morning had been clear, and close on three by the time he made it to Williamson's side.

~

Richard Fleming, Coastal Blockade man, had been stationed a quarter mile west of Williams, also on the opposite bank of the river to Williamson.

"Can you describe the events as they happened?"

"I saw the flash of a pistol and went down to Williams who told me a boat had gone upriver and wouldn't be hailed. So, I too called for the boat to land, but it pulled away. I fired repeatedly, while chasing the boat along the riverbank. It pulled in at Foxholes. Williams asked me to follow him, so I did and swam across the river to reach Williamson and capture the boat."

"Where were the other men at this time?"

"Run away, taking their cart with them. I gave chase but they were too swift."

"Did you know any of the men?"

"I saw no faces I knew."

"And where was Williamson?"

"Lying on the bank, his head cut open. Williams was wrapping his head with a 'kerchief and he told us he'd seen Deaf Tom."

"What was the light level at this time? It was early morning, was it not?"
"It was not very dark nor very light. Williamson might have known a man very well."

"And what have you with you now to show the Court?"

"These here bludgeons, which I found lying near Williamson." He held up three worn bludgeons, blunt and scarred things, battered with use.

The bludgeons were left on the bench for all to see as the story continued to unfold.

Lieutenant Woodham took the stand, a commissioned Officer of his Majesty's Navy, stationed at Crowlink.

"Williamson is a seaman under my orders. His duty was to prevent smuggling. If a boat was to go up the river, he was to prevent her. I stationed him at Foxholes or Cuckmere Haven, where he had orders to stop any boat from smuggling."

The Lieutenant told the Defence, when cross-examined, that he had been some one-and-a-half miles from the spot where the transaction had taken place.

~

Lieutenant Edward Chappell, on examination, informed the court that he commanded the Coast Blockade from Eastbourne to Shoreham.

"In consequence of the prisoner, Mills, being brought to me," Lieutenant Chappell said, reading from a notebook, "I took him to the bedside of Williamson. I enquired of Williamson whether the man I brought before him was Deaf Tom and he replied, "That's the man, I can swear to him, and he can't deny it." The prisoner on hearing this said, "Oh, yes, but his evidence won't do, for my aunt can swear I was in bed from eight o'clock on Saturday night till eight o'clock Sunday morning." At which point I asked him if he was in the habit of sleeping so long and so late, and he replied that he was, unless the tide answered for shrimping."

He addressed the court then.

"The tide answers for shrimping from about one hour before low water till the flood makes. Of course, it must have suited for shrimping at least once between those hours." Referring to his notebook again, the Lieutenant added, "I observed the prisoner's hand which was cut all over and he saw me looking. He said to me, "I suppose you think I got this hand cut there, but I got this cutting wood."

~

Now another Lieutenant came to offer his statement, Lieutenant Henry Sankey: Officer of the Cuckmere Watchhouse.

"I seized the boat, Anne, of Ninfield, and nineteen half ankers of foreign spirits on the morning of August first and conveyed the same to Newhaven Custom House."

~

The Custom's Collector offered up a sample of the spirits and confirmed, along with Lieutenant Sankey, that the gin was of the Geneva variety.

~

Mr. Andrews, for the Defence, offered up several witnesses who could state that Thomas Mills had been in the Old Tree public-house in Seaford at about half-past ten o'clock; and his fellow lodgers saw him go up to bed about eleven.

The presence of these witnesses for the defence bewildered William, who was trying to work out how a man could be at Foxholes, in bed, and at the Seaford tavern all at the same time. He almost laughed out loud when the witnesses contradicted each other about the prisoner's door key and the hat he had or had not had on his head.

Some tradesman of Seaford stepped forward to give the character of Thomas

Mills as harmless and inoffensive, affirming that the man had never been engaged in smuggling, to his knowledge.

~

Mr. Justice Burrough recapitulated the evidence at great length. "In this case, the witnesses for the Crown do not accuse the prisoner of assaulting Williamson, but it is equally a capital offence in the eye of the law to be present with three or more persons, armed with offensive weapons – as is undoubtedly the case here – for the purpose of aiding and assisting in landing goods liable to duties, whether such persons do actually assist therein or not. You, the jury, have heard the evidence on both sides, and it is for you to say whether the prisoner has been sufficiently identified or not."

~

William awaited the jury's verdict outside the courtroom. He thought of those men debating whether to convict the prisoner. It would not be easy for them to convict a man, especially if they were natives of this coast, where smuggling was an institution. The coast had been wilder since the end of the war, too many out-of-work soldiers and sailors struggling to gain employment on farms or in towns – their war-scarred, battle-weary faces did not fit in, scared the children. William himself had found work readily enough with the coast watch, but it could have gone the other way.

~

He was recalled, alone, to the courtroom, where he was asked whether he could swear, again, that the prisoner was the man he saw at Foxholes.

"That is the man, so help me God," he swore.

And again, William waited outside for their decision.

~

He imagined how it would feel for Thomas Mills, sitting in a cell in the same building, waiting for the same decision he himself awaited. Was he preparing himself for the gallows, or hoping the jurors would be less harsh? Wishing fervently to be granted the long journey to Australia's penal colony? William could almost pity the man.

He thought of the Watchhouse at Crowlink and the narrow cleft from the beach straight up to the cliff, from where a narrow valley led directly to the high road and on through the southern counties to London, where the famous Crowlink gin and brandy was sold for a handsome profit in the City's taverns. Despite the manned Watchhouse there, and those at Cuckmere and Holywell, the goods still got through. There was talk in the Admiralty of coastguard cottages to be built near the watchhouses and of a wooden lighthouse to be erected at Beachy Head. The smuggling threat was far from over, the coast far from safe.

~

At last, they were summoned back to the Courtroom. The jury, to a man, watched him hobble in on Fleming's arm. The judge sat in position, impassive. He asked the jurors if they had reached a decision about Thomas Mills. They had. They pronounced clearly and decisively, this time not looking in William's direction at all:

Not Guilty.

Cooper & Sons
1886

astbourne Railway Station was built in 1849 and underwent rebuilds and expansions in 1866 and 1872. The new steam trains brought in a wealth of visitors from the cities, and the town expanded rapidly to accommodate the flourishing tourist boom. Hotels and guesthouses, theatres and promenades, tree-lined avenues and a brand-new pier were constructed to delight the tourists. New roads began to connect the old hamlets of Meads, South Bourne, Old Town and Sea Houses into one single town – Eastbourne. Eastbourne's population surged, along with its popularity, from 3,015 inhabitants in 1841 to 35,000 inhabitants in 1891. By the end of the nineteenth century, Eastbourne had claimed its position as a bustling, fashionable destination, and a forward-thinking seaside town.

This is the story of a boy growing into maturity in a rapidly evolving world, we join him as he learns to navigate the transition from the traditions of the past to the changing fashions and fortunes of his day.

A sign saying *Cooper & Sons*, printed in crisp, cream copperplate on a black wooden board, hung above the door of Ernie Cooper's bootmaker's shop. Douglas Cooper, ten years old, wiry of frame but strong of arm, thought that the sign should say *Cooper & Son,* if it was to be a truthful sort of sign, perhaps he would change it one day, when the shop came to him. He was the son of Ernie Cooper, master bootmaker and leathersmith, and apprenticed to his father while he learned the trade.

His wrists were strong, his hands were well shaped, though his fingers were only as long as they had grown, which was not yet long enough in Douglas's opinion. The leather-working pliers were made for a bigger hand than his, as were the variety of pincers, hammers and cutters hanging from hooks on the walls and scattered across the work bench. They were tools he'd have to grow into.

There were plenty of jobs he could do, with his ten-year-old fingers. He could beat the leather until it was supple; he could polish the boots and keep the workshop tidy, sweep the floor and the lane outside the door; he could wash the windows and climb the ladder to scrub the sign – keep it clear of bird droppings and lichen.

There were times he wondered what else his life might be like, what other skills his little fingers could be turned to – what path his feet would take him on if he followed them out into the world. Did he have the stomach of a butcher, the eye of a tailor or the arm of a soldier?

The soldiers in town – those who had returned from Waterloo – had tales to tell of storms and waves taller than a house, of the weight of cannonballs (heavy) and the smell of gunpowder (eggy), of the sight of ships sinking below the waves. Douglas thought it all sounded heroic. He wondered what London was like and Scotland, he dreamed of America – newly independent and full of promise. Could someone like him find out?

Douglas set out to explore his own surroundings when he wasn't needed in the workshop. He'd run down the mud lane from the shop to the sea and search the rockpools for crabs and shrimp; he'd hunt for shells and smooth-holed stones and rounded driftwood cast ashore by the tide. He was often alone on the beach, apart from the gulls, but he never minded. The hamlets hereabouts were sparsely populated, barely 3,000 souls in all, with acres of farmland in between.

He loved to run along the beach barefoot, his feet splashing in the ebbing tide, and make his way to a gap in the white cliffs where he could scramble up the slope. Ofttimes, he'd run up and down the clifftop slopes until he spotted the Belle Tout lighthouse, where he'd stop and catch his breath, admire the birds, and look out for ships on the horizon. He'd arrive home to find his father busy at the workbench, leather apron smudged with polish, and his mother, sewing in the chair by the window. They would look up and greet him, and carry-on working, their fingers crafting the leather, stitching the seams. They never had a lot, the Cooper's, but they always had enough, and they had enough because of how hard they worked. One day towards the end of his eleventh year, as King George III was succeeded by his son, George IV, Douglas arrived home to such a scene, and knew for certain where his future lay.

His fingers had grown long and slender, his palms had grown wide enough to grip the pliers and hold them tight, they were no longer tools for the future, they were ready for him now. His skills seemed to set themselves in motion from that day on, and Douglas – who had been watching carefully enough over the years – found that he could easily hold the leather taut with the pliers while pushing tacks into the underside of the folded leather. He'd just scraped past his twelfth birthday when he made his first pair of boots, with his father watching on discretely from behind. He worked the pliers and hammers, twisted, and stretched the leather with just enough tension, fastened the leather with tacks and glue and sewed neat stitches along the seams, attached the stiffeners and soles. He worked late into the evening, by candlelight, only stopping when he could do no more. He critically surveyed his work. Five imperfect stitches marred the finish, the upper was a touch off centre, a dab of glue seeped from the sole.

He polished them the next day, with such a buffing that they shone and gleamed. His father joined him at the workbench, patting his shoulder. If a twelve-year-old could make himself a pair of boots in a day, how many boots could a thirteen-year-old make in a day? Douglas decided to find out.

Occasionally, he'd run to the beach to watch the ships sailing in the distance, but he stopped wishing he was on them.

Douglas met Kitty on the seafront, where she was waiting for her father to come back from sea with his usual haul of fish and lobsters. Her dress was plain, apart from a length of good ribbon stitched neatly along the empire-line, and her blue eyes were sad. Her boots were well past their best and looked a trifle small for her, though there was not much of her at all. He waited with her a while, watching the waves rolling in, one after the other, as they crashed on the shingle and retreated.

He met her again a few weeks later, and after that they seemed to see each other whenever they visited the shore. Douglas was smitten and wished to show his affection for Kitty, but all he had to offer was what he could make with his own hands. He stayed up late, working by candlelight to finish a delicate pair of boots in the latest fashion. He shyly handed them to Kitty, who blushed as she accepted them and marvelled at his craftsmanship. Kitty had wanted to be a seamstress, but her family never had enough, her mother took in laundry to wash and that was the closest Kitty ever got to the fine dresses she wished she could make – scrubbing them with suds and hanging them out to dry. Kitty longed to make fine dresses for fine ladies. Kitty was a fine lady, Douglas told her.

A year passed this way.

One day he found her crying by the beach. Her father hadn't come home but bits of his boat had washed ashore. She was going to move to her aunt's house with her mother, but that couldn't last – the house was crowded already. Douglas' house wasn't crowded, he told her. She looked up at him with her big blue eyes, sadder than before, and accepted his proposal.

Douglas was twenty years old when they married at the parish church, Kitty nineteen. He made her a pair of satin wedding slippers, and she borrowed a fine dress from one of her mother's customers. Kitty was never happier than when she moved into the apartment above the bootmaker's shop and she soon settled into a chair next to Douglas' mother, to join in with the stitching.

With the four of them working on the boots, they became known for their speed and fine craftsmanship and their boots were widely sought after – the townsfolk marvelled at the supple leather, the well-formed heels, his mother's neat stitching and Kitty's pretty flourishes.

The next year, their son was born, and George IV died. The day William IV was crowned, Douglas finished making a tiny pair of leather booties for little Jim. He washed the windows and swept the floor and climbed the ladder to give the shop sign a lick of paint.

He packed the tiny booties away in a tin box when little Jim's feet grew longer than the leather. He added another coin (GULIELMUS IIII 1830) to mark the passing year and sealed in a lock of Jim's soft brown hair.

When Little Jim could toddle by himself, Douglas took him down to the beach to play in the surf and hunt for crabs, to build little castles of sand. Douglas loved to take his boots off and roll up his trouser legs to feel the foamy waves sloshing against his ankles. Standing at the sea's edge, he could see all along the coast to the east, right the way round to Pevensey Bay and Hastings beyond. In the other direction, his eyes were drawn to the cliffs at Beachy Head and the long, green ridge of the South Downs. A man was lucky to call such a place home. Helping Little Jim form a flat-topped tower of sand, he pointed out the squat, grey tower on the Wish, a relic from the Napoleonic wars. Sometimes he would walk him down to the Great Redoubt to look at the cannon embrasures and the rounded brick walls. Douglas hoped his boy would never have to fight in defence of his country.

He would hoist Little Jim up onto his shoulders to look out over the vast expanse of blue-green water, two Cooper's with their eyes on the horizon, searching for distant ships plying the channel.

Douglas packed another little pair of booties away in the tin box, with a lacy ribbon wrapped around a curly lock of golden hair. He had made them for Violet, Jim's little sister, but she never had the chance to wear them. Kitty sat in the chair by the window and wept.

The season of sorrow lingered as Douglas's father died and his mother followed soon after. Kitty's mother had passed the year before Violet, and they felt their family shrinking.

Little Jim grew taller and learned to help in the shop, he could beat the leather and polish the boots, sweep the floors, and wash the windows. But Douglas preferred him to stay off ladders.

Kitty sat sewing in the chair his mother used to sit in, she was adept at sewing and the orders came in fast and left quickly. Sometimes she'd take in some dress-alteration work and later, she made time to learn how to stitch fine corsets for the fine ladies of the town. Douglas made Jim a new pair of boots every year.

Little Jim grew taller still and his hands grew well, but they were not yet strong enough to pull the leather tight on the lasts with the pliers. Still, he kept trying, which was all a man could ask of his son. Little Jim went to church school on Sundays and learned his letters and numbers and all the countries of the Empire. Queen Victoria was crowned the year Jim turned eight.

Jim learned to swim in the sea with strong overarm strokes. Douglas would join him and together they would swim out from the shore and along the coast, eyes down for jellyfish and crustaceans, eyes up to the blue-grey sky and white-green hills. Jim learned to catch shrimps and crabs when the tide was out at Splash Point, where the waves rose high above the old sea wall when the incoming tide was blown in by high winds. Kitty would join them sometimes and then she'd walk along the front, past her old rooms at the rear of the Sea Houses hamlet, she liked to look out for the fishermen coming home with their hauls.

Jim's fingers grew longer, and his palms grew wider, and the pliers sat easily in his hands. He stayed up late one evening, making himself a pair of boots and Douglas watched him discretely from behind, patting him gently on the back when the job was done.

The *Cooper & Sons* sign swung unnoticed in the breeze above the new green and white striped awning, the copperplate letters softly peeling away from the weathering wood.

Douglas carefully stitched a tiny pair of booties for Jim's firstborn child, Frank. Jim had married Annie in the parish church in the Old Town hamlet on a fine spring morning in 1849. Cherry blossoms and daffodils bloomed as they walked through the churchyard and in through the fine oak church door to take their vows. A month later, the first steam train pulled into the new wooden station that had been built near Douglas's shop. Nine months later, Frank came into the world, mewling and wailing and setting the apartment above the bootmaker's shop alive with activity.

The shop was alive with activity too, Annie was learning how to stitch neat seams in a chair by the window next to Kitty's and Douglas and Frank worked the leather at the workbench. They didn't have much spare time these days, the trains kept rolling in on puffs of steam with toots of impatience, bringing more and more visitors to the sleepy hamlets and the long shingle coast.

The mud lane in front of the shop was laid over with asphalt, and the paths paved and lined with elms, from the railway station right the way down to the sea, where Lord Burlington, of Compton Place, had built an enormous five-storey hotel near Splash Point and named it after himself. There was a feeling of great change all around, as other roads and streets were built and paved and lined with trees, and the farmlands dwindled to be replaced with large houses, hotels, and guesthouses with sea views.

Trade at the bootmaker's had never been so swift, they worked day and night, hammering and stitching, serving customers from London and Scotland and further afield.

Frank gained two sisters, little Mary, and tiny Faith. Kitty sewed while Annie tended her babes. Douglas made two more little pairs of booties and hired an apprentice to beat the leather and polish the boots, tidy the workshop, and sweep the floor.

War broke out on the Crimean Peninsula. British soldiers joined men from France, Sardinia, and the Ottoman Empire to fight against a Russian attack. The Bourne stream ran foul, bringing sickness and death in its wake as the cholera came and claimed its hold over New Eastbourne. Everywhere there was talk of danger and death and the years ran weary with fright. The cholera left and the war ended, and little Frank turned eight.

The war had an influence on boots, and cardigans - a knitted woollen garment worn by the Earl of Cardigan to keep him warm on long, wintry Baltic evenings in the field. Douglas and Jim began making boots in the newly fashionable military style, while Kitty and Annie stitched the seams and learned how to make crinolines.

Douglas's grandchildren loved to play on the beach, down in the waves at the shore's-edge, making lines of little flat-topped sandcastles and hunting for shells and stones worn right-through. There were pleasure boats plying the water these days, as well as the fishing boats and ships on the horizon. Some days they would climb on board one of the pleasure boats and motor along to the Cuckmere River and back, giggling all the way.

Douglas bought Kitty a mechanised sewing machine a few years after the first model had been patented in America. Kitty bought a new chair to go with a new table by the window that she could set her machine on. Jim and

Annie and the apprentice worked harder than ever.

Frank, Douglas's eldest grandson, was an exuberant child, always on the move. He lived for sport; he loved the speed of football, the accuracy of cricket and the competitiveness of tennis. When he was old enough, he said, he wanted to go to London to seek his fortune, or he talked of going over to America, when the Civil War ended, to start a new life. Nothing could be done to persuade Frank to pick up a pair of pliers, he left that work for the apprentice.

The *Cooper & Sons* sign swung unnoticed from a rusty bracket, with peeling letters and weatherworn wood, and a new crack fracturing its timeworn surface.

Douglas sat in the pale light of the afternoon sun, squinting at a little pair of booties in his hands. It was fiddly work, and his fingers took longer to uncurl than they used to. He scrutinised the stitches, unpicked them, and re-stitched them, twice. Still unsatisfied, he set the little leather pieces down on the table and stretched his arms out above him, yawning. His new great grandchild deserved a decent pair of booties, perhaps he could try again tomorrow.

His granddaughter Mary was expecting. She lived with Jim and Annie and her husband in the apartment above the shop. Douglas and Kitty had moved out a few years before, as the apartment filled with ever-growing Cooper's. Frank had moved to London, with his eyes still drawn to the Americas. Faith lived on the other side of town, in the Meads village, joined now to the other hamlets by long and winding roads. The newspaper informed him that the town had exceeded 10,000 residents, and he did not need reminding about the ever-increasing flow of visitors.

Douglas did not visit the shop so much these days.

When he took a slow stroll with Kitty down to the seafront, they had to share the pavements with a muddle of people and when they stood on the terraced promenade looking out to sea, they had to share the view with a throng of sightseers.

The railway station had been rebuilt and re-sited in the intervening years, a little to the east of its former situation. More platforms now welcomed all the fashionable and distinguished visitors to town on a rolling tide of steam locomotives. The steam was visible above the station for miles around, it lingered over the buildings, hovered over the streets, settled in little grey droplets onto the *Cooper & Sons* sign.

Half of the new pier had been swept away in a storm on the first day of the new year. The remaining half sat marooned offshore, spindly-legged, and forlorn. There was talk of a rebuild and many hoped it would be rebuilt in a more attractive style. Despite the wrecked pier, the Eastbourne waters now hosted innumerable pleasure boats and a paddle steamer borrowed from Hastings and scores of bathing huts and modestly dressed swimmers. Douglas preferred to see the beach in the early morning, before the crowds emerged, when the shingle shimmered softly in the dawn and his only company was a colony of gulls, but Kitty liked to see the crowds, to spot the changing city fashions, and remark on the extravagant bustles, skirt trains, exotic fabrics, and lace-trimmed bonnets she saw.

Out beyond the limits of the pier, over six miles from the shore, the newly established lightship bobbed on the outgoing tide, marking the site of the Royal Sovereign shoal, a submerged rocky ridge famous for its malign presence and the near wrecking of a Charles II warship during the Battle of Beachy Head. He liked to see it there, warding off accident, marking history.

They had seven great-grandchildren by the time the telephone was invented, and Queen Victoria was named Empress of India. It was hard to keep up with all the changes. The older boy, Henry, was showing an aptitude for the workshop, Jim said. He had long fingers and a quick mind, helped no doubt by the free education he was receiving at the local school. Douglas worried that a bootmaker's shop wouldn't keep him satisfied after all that learning, but Jim told him not to mind, that the boy would make his own choice when the time came.

Within three years, the town population had risen to over 21,000 souls. A year later, the new sea wall was finished along with the Royal Parade. Douglas and Kitty carried on in their own way, marking the passing days with a stroll to the seafront and back, marking the passing years with anniversaries and newly minted coins dropped into the old tin box.
There came a day when Douglas could no longer hold the pliers that gripped the leather. He looked at his hands, curled and gnarled, and knew it was time to pack them away – his old pliers and hammers, cutters, and pincers. He packed them in a wooden box and stored them in a cupboard.

On Douglas's seventy-seventh birthday, in the year 1886, a new Town Hall was opened on Gildredge Road. The same year, the newly enlarged railway station was reopened with four platforms and a vaulted ceiling.

Jim and Annie came to visit when they could, and Jim would regale Douglas and Kitty with tales of their new customers and their orders and the latest fashions coming down from the cities. They read them letters sent by Frank from the other side of the world, tales of merchant trading and west coast farming. Mary came sometimes too, with Henry and the little ones and Faith would occasionally stop by. They were content, in their little house, in the ever-growing town.

The words *Cooper & Sons* were almost unreadable on the old sign above the green and white striped awning: the paint had flaked away in the rain and the old sign sighed as the wind blew through.

Douglas sat up in bed, a little tin box on his lap. He unpacked two tiny pairs of booties, one unworn, two tiny locks of soft, fine hair, a lacy ribbon, some seashells, and stones worn-through, a photograph of all the family – apart from Frank and his boys - on a little tin plate, and a bag of coins from each year of his life: four different crowned heads, four different seasons.

Kitty patted his hand and sat next to him, and they gazed fondly at each other, remembering the years as they had lived them. They remembered the wide-open beach and the long-distant horizon; the people walking past their shop through the years – those who stopped by for leather goods and a friendly chat; the boots they had made; the friends they had made; the family they had grown. They had done a lot, and seen a lot in their time, and they were content.

The old *Cooper & Sons* sign broke free from its chains and fell to the pavement below.

Douglas's great grandson, Henry, gathered up the shattered wood and swept away the splinters. He climbed the ladder to take down the old iron bracket that had rusted to the wall.

A fortnight later, Jim climbed the ladder with a screwdriver and screws and a new cast iron bracket to fix to the wall of the shop. He screwed it into the old beam above the awning and hung new iron chains. Henry carried a new sign and passed it up to Jim, who hung it carefully from the bracket.

Cooper & Sons was printed in fresh cream copperplate on smooth black wood and the sign swung gently in the breeze, as the sun dipped down to the west, casting long shadows against the wall of the old bootmaker's shop.

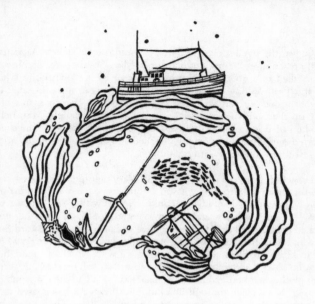

Flotilla for St. Valery
June 1940

The pleasure boatmen and fishermen of Eastbourne were an established community of sailors who could be found daily, plying their trade along the Eastbourne beaches. When the alarm was raised in the last week of May 1940, and the word got around that allied soldiers needed immediate evacuation from the beaches at Dunkirk, the Eastbourne boatmen sent their boats to Dover to take part in the rescue operations. Some of their boats were lost, others returned many days later, pitted with bullet holes and shrapnel. A week later, another alarm was raised. Many hundreds of thousands of allied soldiers had been left stranded in France and still needed help escaping from the Nazi front. The boatmen were once again called upon to lend their boats to the cause, but this time, they would need to man their boats. Meanwhile, soldiers rescued from the Dunkirk beaches were being treated at St. Mary's Hospital, the converted Napoleonic barracks in Eastbourne Old Town.

This is the story of the Eastbourne boatmen's journey to St. Valery-en-Caux, Normandy, in June 1940, and their attempts to rescue allied soldiers from Nazi-occupied France.

It was the smell she noticed first. A meaty, rancid stench that caused a reaction in the back of her throat. Mary Southey steadied herself, pulled in a quick, stealthy breath closer to her own body, which smelt largely of washing powder, disinfectant and sweat, and snipped at the grubby bandage. He was watching her covertly, this French man sitting wearily on the hospital bed, straight from Dunkirk - straight from hell - *l'enfer*, he called it and she could almost see it in his eyes too. The sheets had started out white this morning, starched and crisp, folded neatly at the corners, you wouldn't know it now though.

They'd watched, from the street outside St. Mary's Hospital, with expectant concern as the convoy from Newhaven wound down the hill. The infirmary had filled up quicker than anyone could keep up with. Even Matron was flustered; her cap was askew and there was a streak of blood across her nose. Blackened helmets and dripping boots were discarded across the ward floor along with blood-stained stretchers, rifles, and packs. Men were everywhere, shades of khaki brown-green uniforms stained with blood and mud; boys really, none older than twenty. The smell of war was still on them, lingering on their clothes and bodies. France had fallen, they said, to the Germans and they'd tried to evacuate through Dunkirk, but the Nazis had chased them down, bombed them, shelled them, shot and strafed them. The beaches had been heaving with soldiers trying to get home and strewn with those who never would. Those able to move had waded and swum through the sea to reach boats that had come from England, but the boats were targets too, and many had sunk before their eyes.

"Hold still now." Mary instructed the man. His only response was a slight flutter of his eyelids. When the first maggot fell onto her hand, Mary jumped and the man – "What did you say your name was?" – *Henri* – gazed intently at her before closing his eyes completely. There were things that someone who'd seen all he had seen wasn't willing to see. The man in the bed next to them had only come home with one leg, the other was floating somewhere in the channel, so he thought. Behind them, an Englishman had returned with just half his face. They'd all left something behind in France and Henri she thought, had lost something behind his eyes. Mary excused herself and bustled off for a clean mug to catch whatever else might fall from the bandage. She held it against his leg and snipped. The mug rapidly filled with maggots as Mary forced herself to keep steady. A hand gripped her shoulder and Dr. Herbert McAleenan leant nearer her ear. "Splendid!" he said, as if the maggots in the bandage had been his idea. "They'll have stopped any infections from settling in."

Henri didn't speak to her for a couple of days, though she chatted to him as she changed his bandages and fed him soup. When he did lock eyes with her, it was as though a curtain had been drawn. *"Combien d'hommes avons-nous laissé derrière?"* He asked, as if he didn't want to know. "How many men did we leave behind?"

~

Who would help Police Sergeant Arnold collect the boatmen, the messenger wanted to know? Of course, Mrs. McAleenan volunteered, she'd volunteer for anything important, and her husband Herbert, and son Bill, were still busy inside the Hospital. It was up to her to round the boatmen up, send them on their way. She quickly changed from her nightgown into her day clothes, tied a scarf over her curlers and drove out into the dawn. Five days had passed since the men from Dunkirk had arrived at the infirmary and her husband was still working all hours trying to patch them up, return them to some semblance of their former selves. God knows how he'll succeed, she thought, and offered a prayer into the brightening twilight.

She stopped at each of the houses on the list and roused the occupants, fended off some surprising language and bustled the men into her car, one after the other. She pulled up at the fishing station and sent the men inside. Shivering, for want of comfort, May McAleenan returned home to the flat she shared with her husband above the infirmary ward, but she was past sleep now. She poured herself a pot of tea and worried her way through the early hours. What could those pleasure-boatmen and fishermen accomplish out there on the French coast on their own? Hardy men, she knew them to be, but... she couldn't shake the feeling she'd just sent them to their doom. She only had to look at the men downstairs to know what horrors awaited them.

~

"Glad you could make it men. We've had naval orders from Newhaven – all boats capable of crossing the channel to report there as soon as possible," Police Sergeant Arnold told the men. "Let me note down who's come then you can be on your way."

"Ernest Sayers. Better put Ernie 'Glaxo' Sayers, else no one will know who you mean."

"William Sayers. Call me Bill." Bill winked at Sergeant Arnold, his childhood friend.

"Frederick Allchorn. Fred."

"Prodger. P-r-o-d-g-e-r. Nelson Prodger. Call me Nelson." Nelson grinned as Fred clapped him on the back.

Sergeant Arnold snapped his notepad shut. "Right you are then, you can be off now. The others left at first light so you might meet them over there."

"Others? What others? Who's gone?" Bill asked.

"Henry Boniface.."

"Who else? Sam and Jack Allchorn?"

"Yes they've gone." Sergeant Arnold confirmed, "..and Albert Allchorn. Ned Sayers and Bevan Thornton came early, both the George Erridges, Harry Erridge, Vic Crick and Bert Addington too."

"Gone already, have they? Well, we'd best get ourselves over there too then," Fred said, getting ready to leave.

"Will we be sent home once the Navy have our boats? Like at Dover?" Glaxo wanted to know.

"I can't tell you that, now, I can't. Don't know myself. You'll learn soon enough though, if you're willing." Murmurs of assent passed between the men.

Willing certainly was what the boatmen of Eastbourne were. They'd seen the effects of Dunkirk - lost boats to the evacuation - the Sayers, Allchorns, and Henry Boniface had. Even the Eastbourne lifeboat, the *Jane Holland* had been sacrificed to the Dunkirk rescue. Their small boats had been part of Operation Dynamo, and they'd taken their best boats to Dover where the Navy had commandeered them and sent them over to Dunkirk to ferry soldiers home, while the boatmen had had to make their own way back to Eastbourne. Glaxo would have gone to France then if he could have, had fully expected to.

Since then, they'd heard reports of maimed Dunkirk-survivors recovering at the Old Town hospital, and of course they'd read accounts from evacuees, describing an 'inferno' of German munitions and relentless assaults on the men at the Dunkirk evacuation beaches. The Eastbourne boatmen could imagine only too well what it meant for British soldiers still trapped on the other side of the channel.

~

The horizon had been visible as a line of flame in the distance since they'd left port in the early hours of Tuesday morning. The other crews had left early Monday morning and were already over there... on the edge of God-knew-what. Glaxo found himself scanning the distance, searching for the small boats carrying his friends and family. A futile gesture he knew; it'd take the rest of the morning and half the afternoon to reach the far coast and the rest of the flotillas. The stars faded one-by-one in the gathering dawn as Glaxo kept the *Albion* on course behind the lead-tug that was towing them, Nelson and Fred, and umpteen other fishing boats and pleasure boats from Newhaven and Brighton. They'd been told they were heading for Le Havre and St. Valery-en-Caux. Glaxo and Bill couldn't stop wondering what awaited them there, as they floated inexorably on towards German-occupied France.

Off the coast of Le Havre, in the overhead glare of the mid-summer sun, they approached floating flotillas of small boats and Dutch coasters, the huge

HMS Codrington and several destroyers – two of them Canadian by the looks of it. Away beyond the port, to the west where the coast stretched-out towards the Atlantic, the sounds of explosions could be heard, and a haze of smoke hovered in the near-distance.

"Have you heard?" The skipper of the boat ahead of them called over, "Mussolini's just declared war against us and France." Glaxo whistled, and shook his head, a sensation of futility spreading through him. Bill passed the message back among the other boatmen as Glaxo tried to find out what was going on ahead.

Hundreds and thousands of soldiers had been left behind, they said, hadn't made it to Dunkirk in time; now they were spreading out along the Normandy coast trying to make it home.

Operation Cycle, the Navy were calling this rescue attempt. Men from the 51st Highland Division and a larger allied force had been heading for Le Havre, but the Germans had come between them and forced many of the men to head for St. Valery-en-Caux to try and evacuate there. Tens of thousands of men needed rescuing from St. Valery; the estimates were varied – 50,000 some said – but no one knew how many men had been lost on the journey north.

It hit Glaxo then, that this could go wrong. He counted the boats around him, estimated the capacity of the destroyers, the tugs and schuyts, the fishing boats. It was a good effort, he knew that, but it didn't seem enough. They waited, impatiently, throughout the afternoon, munching sparingly on their iron rations. As the sun climbed down towards the western hills, a motorboat sloughed through the waves towards them. A naval officer greeted Glaxo and Bill and the other volunteers, introduced himself as Admiral William James, Commander-in-Chief from Portsmouth, and bade the men to have good luck and courage, before instructing the tug to tow them to St. Valery, even as a sea-fog swirled in from the east.

The droning-hum of enemy planes signalled their proximity to St. Valery, even before they saw flashes of fire lighting up the town, and heard the staccato-blasts of machine guns echoing round the cliff tops. Cordite-heavy smoke drifted across the *Albion's* prow, mingling with a sea-fog that was following them from Le Havre. Heavy shellfire exploded all along the beaches and cliffs heading into St. Valery, and Luftwaffe planes could be heard whining above them, even before they could be glimpsed through the murky air, dropping their charges over land and sea. The bombing continued unceasingly, rocking the boats as the waves churned wildly under the explosions. As they approached the evacuation point, even Glaxo could see that their little, defenceless boats, wouldn't get to shore.

Through the haze, he glimpsed men running; climbing over rocks on the foreshore; scrambling along the cliff edges; lowering themselves down the sheer chalkface; others standing, waving frantically at the flotilla crews.

Those they could see, the Panzer troops could see too, and before their eyes, men fell, broken, to the ground.

Glaxo instinctively clutched his brother's arm, horror rending him dumb. This was war then. Men of fragile-flesh pitted against metal and fire; lives blotted-out in indiscriminate chaos. *Is it our time to die?* Glaxo thought, and braced himself.

Through the blasts and the missiles, through the smoke and confusion, Glaxo spied two insubstantial boats pushing off from the shore, rowing up to the tug ahead of them. The occupants were helped on board. Endless moments passed until the Sayers brothers saw a cabin cruiser draw up alongside the tug and take the soldiers on board, then draw up next to the *Albion*. Someone tossed a rope over to Glaxo.

"Take these men back to England," the cruiser skipper commanded and eight of the rescued-soldiers crossed over to the Sayer's boat along with a naval rating. Glaxo helped the men aboard, thinking how lucky they were to have escaped the shore, how lucky he and his brother were to be getting out of there. Now towed by the cabin cruiser, Glaxo, Bill, and the new passengers turned away from St. Valery. Not ten minutes after they'd left, enemy planes flew over and dropped a salvo of bombs over the flotilla. Glaxo looked back. "My god, Bill, he has shot the lot!" There was nothing to see but water, hundreds of feet in the air.

As the water sank back to the sea, Glaxo spotted first one, then other boats bobbing about. He counted all he could see. They were all there. The dive-bomber approached again. "Look out Bill!" Glaxo yelled. "It's our turn next!" but the bomber flew straight at the tug and dived for it. The tug's skipper manoeuvred the boat away from the bombs and none of them hit, but the plane came round again, machine-gunning as it passed. The *Albion* crew couldn't see what happened next; smoke and fog swirled behind them, sealing off the coast in a dense, impenetrable curtain.

Night couldn't fall soon enough. The Sayers brothers had eight Frenchmen, sailors and soldiers, on board the *Albion* - seven more had stayed aboard the cabin cruiser. Bloodied and weary, they lay where they had fallen. They were among the last men to be rescued from St. Valery.

Cramped for room, out of rations, and exposed to the chill of the night on the open deck, Glaxo found himself dreaming of a cup of tea. He sat himself down next to a man who looked to be in a bad way. "Tell me your name, boy," he said, holding the man's hand.

"Louis," the Frenchman replied.

"You just hold on there, Louis," Glaxo said. "We'll get you out of here."

Darkest night fell and cleared again, as their small boat rose and fell upon the waves. In between drifted spells of sleep, they watched the sun rise and the Sussex coastline appear on the horizon. Home had never looked so good. But for the Frenchmen, rescued from Normandy, home had never felt so far away.

Most of Ernie and Bill's friends had made it back to Newhaven already. Henry and Ned, and all the others, had been bombed and shot at and though they had tried, over and over, they hadn't been able to get close enough to shore to a rescue a single soul. It weighed heavy on them, the waste, the defeat of it all. Still waiting for news of Fred and Nelson, the boatmen's return to Eastbourne was a quiet one.

~

The morning sun lit the infirmary ward at St. Mary's with a cheery yellow glow. Mary Southey held Louis' wrist as she checked the seconds on her fob watch, before glancing worriedly at his fevered face. She hurried off for Dr Herbert McAleenan.

Henri had made a good recovery, was even walking himself to the bathroom, which was more than could be said of many of the Dunkirk-boys. They'd died, one after the other; the boy with a bullet in his brain; the boy with the head and spinal wounds. Several men had needed amputations, and they'd lost some, the nurses knew, for want of penicillin.

Louis didn't recover from his fever, though it seemed he might for an hour or so, but confusion sat heavy on him until he fell soundly to sleep and beyond. He died just two days after his journey from St. Valery. The other St. Valery survivors recovered in their own time.

The French soldiers had come up from the Somme, where they'd been defending the Maginot Line with the 51st Highland Division, some sixty-odd miles south of the Northern French coast, when the Germans had driven the allied soldiers from Flanders to Dunkirk. They'd marched, with the Highlanders, to Le Havre and St. Valery-en-Caux to evacuate but the Germans had hemmed them in. The French and British forces at St. Valery, having tried and failed to move the evacuation eastwards to Veules-les-Roses, had surrendered the same morning that Glaxo and Bill had returned to Eastbourne.

Around 2,000 British and 1,000 Frenchmen were evacuated from St. Valery before the Germans closed the operation down completely with their incessant fire. The remaining Allied soldiers were captured by Panzer units, some 40,000 men: perhaps 8,000 of them British. From Le Havre though, the Highlanders and other allied soldiers had been evacuated successfully - over 11,000 men were rescued from the German advance.

They listened daily for news on the hospital wireless. They listened to the Germans boasting about their victories, to reports of their advances further into French territory. On 18th June, a message came through from London. General Charles de Gaulle called for the attention of his countrymen. France's politicians were going to sign an armistice with Germany and Italy. The terms were complete surrender. General de Gaulle was offering another solution, a resistance to German occupation

"Henri – what is he saying?" Mary asked quietly. Henri, sitting upright with his ears straining, gestured to another nurse to dial the volume up on the wireless. He listened and offered Mary the odd translated-phrase.

"...Remember this, France does not stand alone... She is not isolated... Behind her is a vast empire... this is a world war... the destiny of the world is at stake... I, General de Gaulle, now in London, call on all French officers and men who are at present on British soil... to get in touch with me... whatever happens, the flame of the French resistance must not and shall not be extinguished." And Henri, whose eyes had held the blankness of defeat since his arrival at St. Mary's, began to kindle that very flame the General talked of, even as tears streamed unchecked down his cheeks.

~

The young French soldier, Louis Marie Diverres, was 27 when he died on the 14th of June 1940, the same day the Germans occupied his home-city of Paris. His funeral was held on the 19th of June, his coffin draped with the tricolour flag and brought to the cemetery at Langney in a slow-moving British Army lorry. British soldiers bore his coffin to the grave site where Glaxo was waiting with his friend, Hugh. The bunch of roses in Glaxo's hand was tied with ribbon and held a card which bore the words 'In honour of a very gallant son of France, from two British Allies, Hugh Newham and Ernie Sayers'.

Beside the boatmen stood two of Louis' comrades from the *Albion*-rescue, Re e Deser, a sailor, with his arm still resting in a sling, and Gabriel Laurent, an infantry soldier like Louis. As the service ended, a British soldier fired three volleys into the air, causing Glaxo to flinch. The buglers followed then, sounding the Last Post across the graveyard, and the echoing call of 'Reveille'.

"Where will you go now?" Glaxo asked Rene and Gabriel.

"To London. I'll join General de Gaulle, someone has to stop these bastards from destroying the world," Rene said.

"The others... they want to go back to France, to surrender like our leaders. But they'll just be slaves to Germany. It's London for me too," Gabriel added. "Resistance all the way."

Glaxo couldn't help but smile. There were some spirits that even war couldn't break. In a church on the other side of town, a young Dunkirk survivor,

Norman Reed, was marrying his sweetheart, Ivy, standing alongside his best man, recovered from Dunkirk too.

The *Jane Holland* lifeboat would soon make a surprise return home from war. Though hit by hundreds of missiles off Dunkirk, rammed and abandoned in the channel, she'd been recovered and towed back to Dover for repairs, and would soon be heading home, along with the *Allchorn's Eastbourne Belle*.

One day, Glaxo thought, the pleasure boats of Eastbourne would line the shore again and the fishing boats would freely ply the sea from Beachy Head to Rye. Perhaps, one day the scars of war would no longer be visible in the landscape; the barbed wire coils and mines dotted along the beach would be removed; the anti-landing scaffolds and concrete anti-tank blocks would be demolished; the anti-aircraft guns would be dismantled; and the military guard could go home. And children would once again know the feel of sand beneath their feet and the lap of water on their ankles.

One day seemed like a long way off but it would come.

Written by Annalie Seaman

Illustrated by Ellie Fryer

Designed by Jamieson Eley

JARROLD
publishing

Published by
Jarrold Publishing
Telephone 01733 296910
www.jarrold-publishing.co.uk